Gone Fishin'...

Florida's 100 Best Salt Waters

Gone Fishin'...

Florida's 100 Best Salt Waters

By Manny Luftglass

Foreword By Kenneth D. Haddad
Executive Director
Florida Fish & Wildlife Conservation Commission

For Tom

Have fun!

12/7/05

Gone Fishin' Enterprises
PO Box 556, Annandale, New Jersey 08801

Pictured on the cover: *(On the left.)* Manny with a 20 pound grouper on the *Blue Heron* out of Riviera Beach. *(In the center.)* Captain Rich Knox of the *Absolute Flats Fishing* out of The Anclote River on the left, with Dr. Tom Callahan holding a 20 pound snook. *(On the right.)* A mate on the *Critter Gitter* from Cape Canaveral releasing a big sailfish. *(In the background.)* A typical Florida sunrise taken by John A. Ward in Boca Raton.

Pictured on the back cover: A load of tanks being added to an Artificial Reef, with reef fish in the background.

Gone Fishin' ... Florida's 100 Best Salt Waters
By Manny Luftglass

© 2004 Emanuel Luftglass

Published By
Gone Fishin' Enterprises
PO Box 556, Annandale, New Jersey 08801

ISBN: 0-9755797-0-3

UPC: 793380 12368 0

Photo Credits:
Florida Fish & Wildlife Conservation Commission, Captain Rich Knox, Capt. Bill White, author Frank Sargeant, Capt. Charlie Wright, Capt. Don Brewer, Capt. Walt Kirschner, Ron Bern, Capt. Skip Bradeen, Bob Sang ("The Reel Guy"), "Tarpon Joe" Greene, Capt. Howard, Dockmaster Grant Stokes, Jack Graham, Capt. Terry Wildey, *Critter* Fleet, Barbara Luftglass-Morea and from the author's private collection.

Design & Typography:
TeleSet
Hillsborough, New Jersey

PRINTED IN CANADA

Let's see,
should I dedicate this book to the ones that got away?
Surely, there have been many of them.
I have had lines snapped
from one end of the state of Florida
to the other by unknown and unseen denizens of the deep,
but I continue to fish
with gear meant to handle smaller critters.

So to the assorted sharks, barracuda,
giant king mackerel and the like
who have done me in, here's to you,
I tip my Gone Fishin' cap to all of you.

But to the fish that are hiding in wait,
hoping that my sissy-sized rod and reel
is the one that presents the next bait offering to you,
I warn you,
I catch enough fish
that you had better not be certain
that you will be "the one that got away!"

Contents

Foreword

By Kenneth D. Haddad

F lorida indisputably owns the bragging rights as the "Fishing Capital of the World." More than 700 world-record catches came from Florida's waters. That's more than any other state can claim. In fact, no other country can touch that record.

Florida offers saltwater anglers 9,800 square miles of fishing opportunities in the Atlantic Ocean, Caribbean Sea and Gulf of Mexico, not to mention the countless bays, bayous, inlets, lagoons and canals. The estuarine environment in Florida is one of the most productive environments on this planet and nurtures an abundance of marine life that attracts anglers from around the world.

Couple the natural reefs with Florida's hundreds of artificial reefs and sound scientific management by the Florida Fish and Wildlife Conservation Commission (FWC) and the result is a system of unparalleled marine habitats. Throw in easy access to the state's waters and Florida emerges as the anglers' wonderland.

An untold array of anglers point to Florida as the place where they bagged the catch of their lives. Florida's waters are warm; fish grow big here. Offshore, barracuda, bonito, sailfish, mackerel, snapper, grouper, and hundreds of other species are hungry and waiting for seasoned anglers and novices alike. Closer to shore, scrappy trout, redfish, sea bass, pompano, cobia, amberjack, snook, mahimahi, flounder, tarpon, and many others await any angler who's looking for a fight.

Fishing is open year-round in Florida, with seasonal closings for some species to allow fish populations to spawn and recharge the resources that make Florida the number one fishing destination in the world.

Fish from a boat or fish from a pier. Fish from a jetty or cast your line from the beach. Fish on the bottom, or fish on the surface — it doesn't matter how or where. You won't be disappointed. That is one of the reasons 80 percent of us who live in Florida make our homes near the coast, and hardly any of us can't drive to a saltwater fishing opportunity within an hour.

Florida offers its waters and marine resources to all, and it does so with the charm, semi-tropical climate, and enchanting scenic beauty that define the essence of the Fishing Capital of the World.

Maintaining Florida's marine and aquatic fisheries requires that sportsmen do their part in the spirit of conservation. If we all are conscientious about taking only what we eat from the resource and leave the rest for another day or another angler, we can help preserve a great heritage.

Equally importantly, we must take care not to pollute Florida's waters with chemicals or discarded fishing line or trash. We invite you to enjoy Florida's natural wonders. We ask only that we all be careful not to leave any scars on its lovely face.

Kenneth D. Haddad, *Executive Director*
Florida Fish and Wildlife Conservation Commission

Author's Preface

"Gone Fishin' ...Florida's 100 Best Salt Waters" is intended for fisherfolk of every age and health (and wealth). I have selected, with lots of assistance, just about every kind of place to fish from. Is your budget restricted? Do you get seasick? We have lots of places that you can stand on solid (or sand) ground and still be able to catch a mess of fish, without worrying about breaking your bank or having to get seasick. You will find inland waterways, piers, bridges, surf spots, and all kinds of offshore sites.

I have given you a wide variety of information sources in the book, like bait and tackle stores, marinas, and captains, including telephone numbers for most of them. Further, you will find on-land directions to most places, and even to a load of boat ramps. Note that I haven't given you more than one or two boat rental operations. Many of these facilities change hands often and, regrettably, some even go out of business, so I haven't provided more than one or two. However, the local *Yellow Pages* will list them and the bait and tackle stores shown herein will also be able to help you find a nearby facility.

And why did I pick "100" sites? Truthfully, I could have picked 100 artificial reefs, and as many natural ones, maybe nearly that many good piers plus surf spots, as well as inland waterways, but I really didn't want to take as much time as that project would have taken. But some day, I may indeed expand the book to 200 when I sell out and have to do my first reprint. If you count carefully though, you may find that this book talks about an extra 20 or so places, anyway!

So to all of you who want to fish the spectacular waters found in the great state of Florida, here's wishing you lots of luck in your search for the beast of your choice at the venue you seek your prey in. I hope that you will learn enough about the state by reading this book that you will know where to go and what to do when you get there. Florida! From the Westernmost Gulf down to the Keys and then wrapping around and way up to the northeasternmost part of the state, read on, and I hope you enjoy it along the way.

According to the *Florida Statistical Abstract of 2000,* the coast-line of Florida includes 8,426 miles. But please note that when I talk about on the water mileage to a place in the book, even if I don't repeat it each and every time, I mean "nautical" miles. As just noted in the previous paragraph, we will tell you in geographic sequence about the state. I will identify locations by area/county in the table of contents. I would like you to know that I would rather fish the saltwaters of Florida than those I have fished in not less than ten other states (and countries). Florida offers so much more than elsewhere, and maybe near the top of my "why Florida?" list is the air temperature! I love it!

One other note — besides all of the folks that I list as information sources within the locations themselves, I also went to my copies of the DeLorme Atlas and of Frommer's map of Florida to find my way around many of the state's waterways. And for assistance in identifying one fish from another, I got a copy of *Sport Fish of the Atlantic* by Vic Dunaway, published by *Florida Sportsman.* And Frank Sargeant's fine book, *Secret Spots — Southwest Florida,* published by Larsen's Outdoor Publishing, was also quite useful to me.

Who To Thank

I will not name each and every person who contributed assistance to me because, for sure, I will certainly insult a few by not listing them here. But you will see the names of the some of the folks who lent a hand at each such location. Without doubt though, there are a few who work for the state who stand out. First and foremost was Ken Haddad, Executive Director of the Florida Fish & Wildlife Conservation Commission. I will refer to the commission often within the book. So however I write it, "Fish & Wildlife," "Commission," etc., please know that I am referring to the good guys and gals of that entity. And for certain, some of the people in Ken's staff who gave me enormous assistance include (I will omit their titles if that's okay with you) — Scott Willis, Jon Dodrill, and in particular, Bill Horn. Without these four men, the book would have missed the mark that I was trying to reach!

Rules And Regulations

I am going to cop out here for good reason. There are so many rules and regulations that change so often that it really makes no sense to provide you with a list of fish that have bag, season, and size limits. You see, as with the tide, things go in and out. Was a red/pink porgy (a/k/a "Rose Perch") ever illegal to keep? Or did it ever have a size limit? Since both rules have applied at separate times, I am going to take a pass. Ditto Queen triggerfish — Illegal to keep or size limit? How many snappers of which size can you keep? Which groupers have size limits and what are they? Many other fish have their own restrictions, of course.

Truthfully, it makes no sense to quote such restrictions since they change from time to time, based on available supplies. And to complicate things much further, Federal law takes over beyond a certain distance from either coast, Gulf or Atlantic. No matter what you read herein, to know what is in and what is not, I must refer you to the guy with the most knowledge, your Captain! But if only for back-up, I suggest you contact the State and request a copy of the current *Florida Recreational Saltwater Fishing Regulations,* by writing to Florida Fish & Wildlife Conservation Commission,

Division of Marine Fisheries, 2590 Executive Center Circle East, Tallahassee, Florida 32301. This booklet will also list Florida's saltwater licensing rules. Check it out, please.

Artificial Reefs

Florida may have more artificial reefs then any other seashore state in the whole country. The state itself has done a spectacular job. The state has been aided by local and federal government, as well as by members of the private sector. People and businesses have contributed dollars to clean up and tow out every kind of object imaginable. Fishing groups, boat captains, and fishing related businesses, have all gone out of their way, as have breweries, electronics companies, fishing line companies, magazines, etc. The list goes on and on. A contribution in the name of a deceased loved one has been a common method of raising necessary funds. The bottom line though is that the bottom is literally "lined" with structure that has been added from the "Panhandle" down to the "Keys," and clear up to the border with Georgia! And to those folks who have played a part in this forward thinking, my gratitude is endless!

Can I Eat It?

Okay, here comes Manny with another "cop-out!" You see, this book was not intended to teach you what kind of fish are good to eat and which aren't. For certain, it will not provide warnings about Ciguatera or mercury or any other form of toxin. Which are "safe" to eat and which aren't? That's where the health department of your area comes in.

Can I Touch It?

No, don't touch a scorpion fish. It can sting badly, and maybe even send you to a hospital. Ditto a catfish, unless you really know what you are doing. Stargazers may be nice to look at, but don't touch 'em! And if you have ever been sliced by the gill plate of a squirrel fish, you know to leave that one to the mate. There are many fish that can hurt you badly. For example, a moray eel will literally go after you with its mouth open, ready to bite. So if you get one on, cut your line! Hesitate on the side of caution if you have never seen the fish that you are about to haul into the boat. And if the mate doesn't know what it is either, it may be time to practice "Catch and release," with scissors!

How Do I Get There? (Electronics)

I am hopelessly brain-dead when it comes to things mechanical. I still tell people that all that I know about the computer on my desk is that it is GRAY. Yes, I had an "Eagle" fish finder on my little boat that I replaced with a Lowrance X65, but do I know how they work? Not! And while I use the machine to find depth and maybe to see what level the fish are swimming at, I sure am clueless regarding any of the technical stuff. But in order to please you who want to know where a place is and how to get there, I turned to the experts who I talked to so as to be able to show you the "Numbers!" But do I know "numbers" and what they mean as they relate to GPS or Loran from latitude and longitude? Hey, no, I really don't, and since I do most of my fishing on board party and charter boats, it really doesn't matter to me one iota. But again, to satisfy you machinery wizards, I turned to Lowrance Electronics, Inc. to provide translations. You will see that I probably listed the "numbers" for three-quarters of my "100 Best" locations that are offshore. A handful of them involve the use of LORAN (LOng-RAnge Navigation). It's a navigational system similar to GPS (Global Positioning System), except it's based on ground radio transmitters.

And now let's hear from Steve Wegrzyn of Lowrance to help translate "Numbers" for us.

"Finding a location by GPS, by the numbers-the lat and the lon of it. An "address" is a wonderful thing. It gives you a locational reference to find any house, any business, and really, any place populated by people" (writer's note-or fish). "The "address" is the location's Latitude and Longitude, and is expressed in modern terms as simply "lat/lon." If you know the lat/lon of a place you want to find you can use a paper map of the world and get reasonably close to the location. However, using a GPS, you can find a lat/lon with a lot more precision, as well as a lot faster.

So what exactly is a Latitude and a Longitude?

They are hypothetical (invisible) lines that encircle the Earth, vertically and horizontally, and form a grid pattern. Latitude lines make parallel circles around the globe running east and west. Longitudes are lines running north and south and meet at the poles. Both Latitude and Longitude are measured in degrees, minutes, and seconds. (note from Manny) — LORAN numbers will be shown in the book as four digits, a period, and then several more numbers. I will use the numbers that the State gave me for their artificial reef sites, namely four numbers, a period, and then three more. Lowrance told me that there are several methods of identification available via GPS. One such numbering system involves two numbers, representing degrees, followed by a degree sign (°) and then two more, representing minutes, and then three more, representing seconds."

"A GPS that's activated and has acquired satellite signals will not only display your current location and direction of travel via an icon (like an arrowhead). It should also display your lat/lon at every step of the way. And if you have lat/lon coordinates you're wanting to find, you can do that with relative ease and speed." You can get to a predetermined location or mark a new one for future reference.

I will not get into the more technical side of this subject but suggest instead that you who want to use your own boat to find the locations in this book take a Coast Guard safety course. Do this especially if it involves navigation, and pick up a GPS machine for your boat — if you don't have one already.

A few of the Lowrance machines that are available (this is NOT an endorsement of Lowrance products, I list them simply for you who want a couple of ideas) — are:

A portable, hand held unit (NEVER take this on board a party or charter boat to steal "numbers" or else risk life, limb, and your machine too) — the iFinder H20 — it should cost well under $300. Next comes a unit that you mount on your boat — a GlobalMap 3300c — this is a bit over $500 at retail. Last but not least is the 10+ inch diagonal screen that is found on the GlobalMap 7000c — at $1,899 retail, costly, but effective.

You can use a GPS to bring you to a location that you want to reach but also to mark a spot that you discover yourself. Say you are out fishing and you run into a mess of bottom fish. Your sonar device shows fish galore and wreckage that isn't on any charts you own. It may be tough to do, but stop fishing, and use your machine to "mark" the spot in memory for future reference. Punch in the site and memory will hold this spot for you. Make sure to have a waterproof paper notebook to record a spot that you saved into memory with your own code. GPS can be used to get you to a location found in your book, and also to mark new ones. Don't rely on the machine for navigation though, think of it only as a device to bring you to fish!

Locations
1 — Gulf Coast

1) PENHALL REEF . . . . .Pensacola
2) DOUBLE TROUBLE . . . . .Pensacola
3) THOMAS HAYWARD REEF .Destin
4) THE EMERALD COAST PIERS . . . . Pensacola Beach
                                       through Panama City Beach
5) OPAL BEACH . . . . .Opal Beach
6) STAGE 1 EAST — HATHAWAY REEF . . . . . .Panama City
7) COMPASS ROSE . . . . .Carrabelle
8) D-DOG . . . . .Carrabelle
9) Law Reef . . . . .Carrabelle
10) MARKER 24 BARGE REEF . . . . . . .St. Marks Lighthouse
11) STEINHATCHEE REEF . . . . .Steinhatchee

12) CITRUS FISH HAVENS (3) . . . . .Crystal River
13) PINE ISLAND .Hernando Beach
14) A. H. RICHARDSON ("FISH HAVEN") REEF . .Hernando
Beach
15) PASCO ARTIFICIAL REEF . . . . .Tarpon Springs
16) TARPON SPRINGS REEF . . . . .Tarpon Springs
17) PASCO TWO ARTIFICIAL REEF . . . . .Tarpon Springs
18) RUBE ALLYN REEF . . . . .Tarpon Springs
19) HONEYMOON ISLAND/NORTH END . . . .North Dunedin
20) DUNEDIN REEF . . . . .Dunedin
21) CLEARWATER REEF . . . . .Clearwater
22) BLACKTHORN . . . . .Clearwater
23) THE SHERIDAN . . . . .Clearwater
24) THE SEVENTY FATHOM PEAKS . . . . .Bradenton
25) THE MIDDLE GROUNDS . . . . .Bradenton
26) MIDDLE GROUND (FLAT) . . . . .Sarasota Bay
27) "POINT OF ROCKS" .Sarasota
28) "M-1" . . . . .Sarasota
29) VENICE INLET . . . . .Venice
30) GASPARILLA PASS/SOUND . . . . .Placida
31) PHOSPHATE DOCKS . . . . . .Gasparilla Island (South End)
32) BOCA GRANDE PASS . . . . .Charlotte Harbor
33) BOCA GRANDE BAR . . . . . . .Offshore of Charlotte Harbor
34) CHARLIE'S REEF . . . . .Boca Grande
35) EDISON REEF . . . . .Sanibel/Fort Myers Beach
36) BIG LEDGE . . . . .Fort Myers Beach
37) STONY POINT . . . . .Fort Myers Beach
38) NORTHWEST BOTTOM . . . . .Naples
39) SOUTHWEST BOTTOM . . . . .Naples
40) EMPRESS HONDURAS AND OILER WRECKS . . .Naples
41) GORDON PASS . . . . .Naples
42) ROOKERY BAY . . . . .Marco Island
43) PICNIC KEY FLAT . . . . .Everglades City
44) WATERMELON PATCH .Chokolosekee ("10,000 Islands")
45) SNAKE BIGHT . . . . .Flamingo

2 — The Crown Jewel
46) THE DRY TORTUGAS

3 — The Keys
47) BOCA GRANDE BAR ....Key West
48) WESTERN DRY ROCK ....Key West
49) SEVEN MILE BRIDGE ....South of Marathon
50) HAWK'S CHANNEL ....Marathon
51) "2038" ....Marathon
52) DAVIS REEF ....Islamorada
53) ISLAMORADA HUMP CHANNEL ....Islamorada
54) MIKE'S LEDGE ....Key Largo
55) THE DUANE ....Key Largo
56) SPIEGEL GROVE ....Key Largo

4 — The Mighty Atlantic
Biscayne Bay Flats
57) BLUE FIRE Key ....Biscayne
58) THE PIPE/BUBBLER ....North Miami Beach
59) ANDRO ....North Miami Beach
60) DUMBFOUNDLING BAY ....North Miami/Aventura
61) BUOY ONE ....Fort Lauderdale
62) THE MERCEDES/REBEL DRIFT ....Fort Lauderdale
63) THE SLAB ....Fort Lauderdale/Pompano Beach
64) LOWRANCE/MAZON REEF ....Pompano Beach/
Fort Lauderdale
65) SNOWY GROUPER LAND ....Pompano Beach
66) THE DELRAY OUTFALL ....Delray/Boynton Beach
67) VERMILION ALLEY ....Offshore of Boynton Inlet
68) OFFSHORE OF LAKE WORTH PIER ....Lake Worth
69) LAKE WORTH PIER ....Lake Worth
70) LOST TREE VILLAGE ....Juno
71) OFFSHORE OF JUNO PIER ....Juno
72) HOBE SOUND LORAN TOWER REEF .....Hobe Sound
73) PECK LAKE LEDGE ....Gomez/Hobe Sound
74) THE KINGFISH NUMBERS ....Stuart

CHAPTER 1

The Gulf Coast

#1 "PENHALL REEF"
Pensacola (Escambia County)

L et's start off with one of the wonderful sites that exist in Florida that was "created" rather than existing courtesy of nature. As you ramble through the 100 specific locations found in this book, you will see many that have been in place forever. But lots of them were established because of an accident, maybe an act of war, but more likely, the result of an intentional sinking of material put into place to create fish havens. Clearly, the "Penhall Reef" is one of the largest placements of material into a single area.

The old Blackwater Bridge was taken down in February of 2002 and its rubble was cleaned up and taken by barge to a point that sits 14.7 nautical miles offshore of Pensacola Pass. Again, this may be the largest deposit of material at one site, because 5,700 tons of material went over to the bottom and quickly, nature took over the process of creating an artificial reef.

Snapper form the majority of the fish that are caught out on the Penhall Reef, with three varieties being the ones most caught. Red snapper, the most popular member of the snapper family to restaurant patrons, are at this huge chunk of bottom. And, of course, as an aside, it's possible that 75% of the meals purchased at restaurants clear across the land that feature "red snapper" may really be selling you some other kind of snapper, but let's forget about that for now.

Vermilion snapper, clearly a snapper that is distinctively red in color (but not a "red" at all) is number two. And taking up the rear is the overbite family member, mangrove, which are commonly called "gray" snapper in many parts of Florida.

The biggest snappers are usually the real "reds" and to get them, a large hook and bait is the norm. Mangroves will eat the same offerings, of course. And while a vermilion may want to eat the same bait, they are generally much smaller and a 6/0 hook with whole live bait will scare most of them off. So for vermilions, we suggest you go with a double hook set up and smaller baits.

Penhall lies on bottom in 92 feet of water and has a 12-foot profile. It's found at latitude 3005.523 Longitude 8711.497. And remember, mechanical wizards, this numbering system may differ from those used by your machine but again, wherever I use lat/lon, note that the actual numbers will be correct but that the placement of degrees signs, period placement, etc., will differ.

#2 "DOUBLE TROUBLE"
Pensacola

We should all have such double trouble! This location has this name because the wreckage of two cars that were sunken offshore some years ago make up the basic material of the spot. This site has been added to by the placement of other rubble and all in all, if not fished too often, is considered a dependable place to find fish.

The Southwind Marina also houses Ryan's Catch Restaurant (1-850-492-0333) and as with a few other places that I've visited, arrangements can be made to bring your cleaned fresh-caught fish in and they will cook it up any style you want, right on the spot.

If you have never tried a fillet of triggerfish that was caught only a few hours earlier, don't forget to visit this marina and book a trip on one of the nearby boats. Have the mate clean your fish and get thee quickly to the restaurant for a meal for a lifetime.

You can get to *Double Trouble* on a local boat by sailing approximately 22 miles south of the Pensacola Inlet. Although wreck fishing is done in Florida on anchor, Lynn Woodruff (who works at the Marina) told me she usually drifts this area for top results.

The primary fish sought are grouper, black and red, with more reds prevailing. True red snapper are on the bottom, along with triggerfish that are commonly caught down there too. Amberjacks swim up off bottom, wherever they can find something to eat, and if you are reeling up from bottom and suddenly get slammed, chances are good to excellent that it was an "A. J." that gotcha! Most of the amberjacks are half-way down or even higher up.

This is deep water, upwards of 120 feet or so, so forget the light and whippy rods. Fish with live bait if you can get some, using a large single hook in say size 7/0 or so with a long leader below your heavy egg sinker. Whole frozen squid will do business too, and a large chunk of fresh cut baitfish will do the trick, but you may be bothered by smaller fish. If triggerfish are your goal, at least part of the day, then go with two snelled size 2/0 hooks, one above and the other below a bank sinker. Make sure the sinker is tied with an easy to break knot so that you can snap it off and retrieve a fish that got your sinker stuck in wreckage. Live hardtails, a small silvery fish shaped like a pompano, are local favorite baits, especially to the amberjack anglers.

BONUS SITE — *THE USS ORISKANY*

And while we are talking about the Pensacola area, let's give you a head's up about a site that is sure to become a spectacular reef. It's just too soon to list it because her addition to the bottom of the gulf may actually coincide with the publication date of this book!

The 884-foot retired aircraft carrier *Oriskany* was to be sunk 22 miles southeast of Pensacola in 212 feet of water sometime in 2004. The *Oriskany* served in Vietnam and one of her crew members was Sen. John McCain who was taken prisoner in North Vietnam after taking off from the ship in 1967.

One of the reasons that Pensacola was chosen as the site for the sinking was because the ship had had a role as a pilot training base. And when sunk, she would become the largest vessel deliberately sunk in the United States to become a reef. But it is quite probable that larger ships yet would be put down somewhere else later on, including three other aircraft carriers.

#3 "THOMAS HAYWARD REEF"
Destin (Okaloosa County)

Here's another artificial reef, the Liberty ship "Thomas Hayward," which went to the bottom in the spring of 1977. She was 369 feet in length and rests on bottom 90 feet below the surface. She's a large wreck with a profile of 25 feet and offers a variety of structure for several kinds of fish to call home.

This spot is reached only 6.5 nautical miles from Destin Pass, and is at latitude 3018.376, longitude 8636.222.

Red snapper are the primary fish being targeted but don't forsake the large numbers of triggerfish that reside at the Hayward. In fact, you may want to fish for snapper first and then switch over for triggers later in the trip.

Since so much steel awaits you below your boat, you may want to fish with a breakaway sinker. Depending on current movement, use the lightest sinker that can take you directly to the bottom. You will not want any belly in your line caused by an undersized lead because that will usually result in you getting hung in bottom and breaking off.

Tie your line onto a three-way swivel and affix a heavy fluorocarbon four-foot leader to the second loop, with a size 6/0 non-offset hook. Now add a one-foot length of 20 pound mono to the third loop with an overhand knot and add in your sinker, with a second overhand knot.

The idea here is to hook a fish that may bring you into the wreckage but if luck is with you, only your sinker will hang badly. The light leader as well as the easy to break-off overhand knot may result in you losing your sinker often. However, you will be reeling up fish even more often instead of losing them to the structure.

Triggerfish will eat anything that isn't about to eat them. So go

'Jacks like these are often found at the Hayward Reef.

with a size 2/0 or 3/0 hook, maybe two in fact, with a hunk of squid as bait. Remember the size limit and please don't take too many home. It will be difficult to get your unknowing neighbors to accept uncleaned triggerfish and in fact, unless they know how to clean them, most friends will no longer answer their door when they know it's you with some triggers. But to those of us who know how? Oh my, what fine eating indeed!

And last but not least on the wreck of the good ship Thomas Hayward are those bundles of lightning that swim up higher in the water column, amberjacks. While they will certainly take an offering of bait, I suggest you hang a four to six ounce Ava style jig half-way down to the bottom and jig it up and down for a few minutes. You may find that your lure is inhaled as it settles down at the bottom of the lift and gets very, very lively all at once. Most "A-J's" will hit on the fall rather than on the lift of the jig.

#4 THE EMERALD COAST PIERS

I turned to Tim Broom who manages the Half-Hitch Tackle store in Destin (1-877-369-4360) for information and he sure was helpful. Instead of selecting a single pier for you, let's discuss the series of four most popular ones that cover the "Emerald Coast," and they run from the west to east, in this order:

First comes the Pensacola Beach Pier. (850-934-7200). And then we have the Navarre Pier. (850-936-6188). Then, at Fort Walton Beach, is the Okaloosa Island Authority Pier. (850-244-1023) Last but not least is the easternmost one of the string of four, the well-known Dan Russell City Pier in Panama City Beach. (850-233-5080). There certainly are more piers in this wide range of territory but arguably, these may be the best. Of course if you can prove that there are several others, I may have to come out with a second edition of this book, covering the 125 "best" some time later.

All four piers have showings each season of blackfin tuna. You can just imagine what can happen to the nerves of an unsuspecting angler when one of these balls of lightning slams into a rod. No doubt a tight drag on a propped up rod means one of two things: either a broken line or a rod that flies into the air like a free-jumping sailfish. And on that note, Tim added that each pier is visited by a few sails every year as well. For sure, more blackfins are taken than sailfish, but one never knows when such a critter will attack.

The best of the cobia fishing found on the Emerald Coast Piers occurs at the Pensacola Beach Pier. Try live-lining a bait-fish that you just caught for the cobia. Chuck out a whole squid too on the outgoing tide side of the pier and a cobia might prefer that for its last supper. Spanish mackerel are taken here by guys throwing jigs. If safe enough (it isn't a nice thing to hook a neighbor in the head, nosirree), rig with a weighted jig with two colored feather teaser hooks above the jig for the mackerel.

Pompano are the target species at the Navarre Pier but lots of other fish are taken also.

Half-Hitch has special rigs for pompano. We will talk about them when we discuss Opal Beach.

Next in line is the Okaloosa Island Pier Center where kings replace Spanish mackerel as the primary fish of choice. From March 1st on until the first or second hard freeze occurs, generally in December, king mackerel are sought and caught at this site in goodly number. Stout rods are required with at least 20 and maybe more like 30-pound line a must. A steel leader is helpful to avoid being cut off by the razor sharp choppers found in their nasty mouths. As with all big fish, live bait works best. But a whole or even a half of a sardine often produces good action from the kings. Make sure you know the bag and size limits for these fish because they do change from time to time.

And the easternmost of the four piers is the well-known Dan Russell Pier at Panama City Beach. Here again, it is the Spanish variety of mackerel that are most commonly found. But don't dismiss the fact that a sailfish might inhale your Spanish and take it for a ride. In addition, a torpedo-shaped blackfin tuna is always a possibility so if you are fighting a modest-sized fish and all of a sudden a freight train charges away with it, be prepared with an open drag or get ready to re-rig.

#5 OPAL BEACH
Opal Beach

Yes, getting on a boat and heading way out to sea, be it the Gulf or the Atlantic, is something that many of you will prefer. But for the weak of stomach and maybe the smaller of bankrolled anglers, we have selected some spots for this book that guarantee a few things. First is that you won't get sea-sick and second is that you won't have to hock your socks to pay for the adventure. The Emerald City Piers are certainly a fine example of this and so too is Opal Beach.

Tim Broom of Half-Hitch Tackle (1-877-369-4360) is the manager of their store in Destin. He might be better as a spokesman for the city of Destin because he told me that in his opinion, Destin offers "the best overall fishing in the world!" WOW! In further explaining this, he added that for sure, better mackerel action might be elsewhere, ditto sails, and for certain, grouper and snapper catches are more common at other ports. But for combined results of all saltwater species found in Florida, he feels that this area is tops. Tim said that the Destin area has more charter boats than in Miami and W. Palm Beach combined.

And for a surf fishing area, he suggests Opal Beach! Pompano are the fish of choice from this enormous stretch of sand. It's within the Gulf Island National Seashore Park, between the cities of Navarre and Gulf Breeze. Free parking is available six months of the year as well. The warmer times involve a modest charge.

Top action on pompano takes place from 3/15 to 6/1 or so. The area involved is huge too so don't worry about competing for a spot with another angler. Just take your sand spikes and a little chair and get ready for fun.

Besides pompano, whiting and redfish are commonly caught. Cobia invade the suds each spring and live eels work best for them. Some cobia are also caught on whole squid. And if you aren't scared of the dark, night action sometimes involves shark catching!

For pompano, Tim sells a special rig that they carry. It's custom built and offers a fluorocarbon leader with two size #2 circle hooks and a colored "floatee" above the hook eye (to take your bait off bottom and away from crabs). A sinker that is painted with the same color as the floatee often adds to the action. Orange and pink are the favored colors.

#6 STAGE 1 EAST — HATHAWAY REEF
Panama City

Check out your Atlas in Panama City and you see that a bridge crosses over the intracoastal to Panama City Beach. The road numbers are 98 and 30 and the name of the bridge is the Hathaway Bridge. And my guess is that some serious construction, or maybe I should say "re-construction," took place at this site back in 1988. That's because 80 tons of concrete bridge slabs were barged out into the gulf and dropped overboard by a crane after having been properly cleaned up.

This form of recycling isn't anything new, of course. It's been going on all over the east coast for 30 years or so. I remember when the program first began in New Jersey and cannot swear which state actually started it, but many joined quickly in. Back then, party and charter boats were the first to assist in New Jersey. Boy Scout troops joined with fishermen and builders to create artificial reefs. We have come a long way since then, of course, but I can still remember nearly herniating myself as several of us would lift these huge airplane tires up over the stern of the Miss Point Pleasant and plop them down as additions to the Sea Girt Reef. The tires had holes punched in them so that they could easily sink, and were wired together. Concrete plugs were stuck into the tire openings to assist in getting and holding them down at bottom.

And then someone came up with the idea of sending bridge and highway material down. And somewhere in the process, the military lent their assistance, by volunteering old, obsolete equipment like tanks and the like. Well, the Hathaway reef is just one of many examples of how room can be saved in the garbage dumps all at the same time as the material is being made quite usable at sea!

You can reach this Bay County site by sailing 11.4 nautical miles out of the St. Andrews Pass to latitude 2956.663, longitude 8549.196. The pile sits up off bottom by eight feet in 96 feet of water. And the main fish that people are seeking are amberjacks. No, they may not be as big as the beast that you will see a picture of that was caught down off Islamorada, but still, an amberjack is indeed a fine fish to catch and plenty of them swim up above the Hathaway Reef.

Gag grouper are the most popular of the bottom fish that are at this site and some guys swear that the use of a live grunt is the way to catch the bigger groupers. For sure, live pin fish may be the best bait of all but you will have an easier time finding grunt at this site. Use as little as a two foot leader below your egg sinker and be sure to have a stiff action rod. As soon as you feel that heavy tug, slam back and crank as fast as you can. The result just might be a fine meal for two (or more) members of your family. Fresh grouper? It cannot be beaten, for sure.

Triggerfish are the most commonly caught food fish that swim in this area, and they come in all sizes. Since they have few enemies due to their very tough skin, you may find schools of smaller fish rising to the top if you drop enough bait over. But most of the keeper-sized fish are at bottom, just waiting for you to present some bait to them.

#7 COMPASS ROSE
Carrabelle

"Compass Rose" isn't really the name of this large area of productive bottom. But when Captain Randy Craft of the good ship *Debo Too* (1-800-897-7106) told me about it, I figured we may as well hang that moniker on it. You see, when Randy runs his boat out of the Carrabelle Inlet, he often points it towards a huge section of rocky bottom that can be found right under the Compass Rose portion of NOAA chart #11405, thus the name, got it?

This area is found 6-7 miles south of the inlet, below Dog Island, and is really loaded with underwater caves and springs which present numerous hiding places for grouper to rest and wait for passing prey.

The water ranges from 30-45 feet in depth and a variety of fish call the bottom home. Sea bass may be the most commonly caught critters here and, of course, they will eat simply anything presented to them. But if I had my 'druthers, I would 'druther offer them a chunk of oily mackerel. Yes, squid will do, and even shrimp if you have a friend who has some to spare. But a simple hunk of mackerel on a size 2/0 or 3/0 hook will produce sea bass and still be big enough to catch a larger fish. Most of the sea bass here won't really present a serious battle, but do they taste good? Oh my, they sure do.

If you are so inclined, try for grouper on this spot with a modified circle hook, offset, in size 6/0, with a large piece of bait. A live grunt may be your best bet. You just need to know that you will get very few bites on a grunt, but when you do, be ready to stick, lift skyward, and reel in a hurry to get the grouper away from its favorite cut-off rocks.

There's a boat ramp near the southeast end of Carrabelle Beach but again, it's safer to charter a boat.

#8 "D-DOG"
Carrabelle

Called D-Dog because this reef is found south-east of Dog Island (maybe 7½ to 8 miles away), the *Debo Too* fishes here with

Reefballs being placed on a Carrabelle artificial reef.

frequent success. We referred to NOAA chart #11405 above. Buy a copy if you intend on fishing these waters by yourself, but of course, as I will preach to you throughout this book, you would be better served if you hire a captain to take you out in his charter boat. Where available, headboat skippers are a fine alternate.

One excellent hunk of this reef is found on Randy's Sitex Loran C machine at 14378.9/46440.6. Grunt, the ever-present bait stealing but quite edible fish, are here in huge numbers. Called "Ruby Lip" snapper by some because their inner lip is truly bright red in color, the best way to avoid reeling up grunt after grunt would be to go with big bait and hooks. But if you want to catch some for bait, or maybe to please the youngster you brought with you, go small for a while until he or she has had enough. Then get serious into catching sea bass on larger hooks, or maybe grouper, the ones you really are after anyway, right?

The bottom here consists of coral and limestone ledges, and you will find 38 feet of water under the boat when you drop to the bottom. Gag grouper are most common but red grouper reside alongside. At times, you may catch as many as 70% keepers to 30% undersized fish here, particularly in the early spring.

"L-Y's," the local nickname for menhaden/mossbunker, make wonderful bait for everything. But a package of frozen tinker mackerel, ranging from 8-10 inches, will usually work better for bigger fish. Try half of a mackerel on a 40 inch leader below your eight ounce egg sinker. For grouper hooks, go big but not long shank — say a 5/0 to 7/0. Make sure the steel is strong, not one of those Aberdeen style, unless you want to have a straightened hook in a heartbeat.

#9 LAW REEF
Carrabelle

Capt. Craft runs a south by southeast course to get to this area of ledges and hard bottom. It sits in 47 feet of water and runs for a considerable distance from west to east. Several boats can fish it at the same time since it extends 400 or more yards.

A mid-point loran reading would be 14375.3/46392.1, and the ever present sea bass are still the main fish you will find, but since this is 14 miles or more from the Carrabelle River Inlet, you may want to forget about grunt and sea bass and try for bigger critters.

Grouper still are the main big fish to look for, but at this section of bottom, two of the best fighting and finest eating snappers will usually be on hand. True red snapper are here and this is pretty close to shore for them, but present they will be! Just be sure that you are up on your size and bag limits because red snapper are perhaps more highly regulated than any of the large snapper caught in Florida. "Black" (best known as "Mangrove but also referred to often as "gray") snappers are the other snappers at Law Reef.

While a mangrove is often very wary and requires you to use an extra long leader to fool them into eating your offering, for some reason, they are not as finicky on this reef and a standard three to four foot leader is all you should need.

Also present at this spot are triggerfish. If you want them, you may have to go with a smaller hook. Triggers have a very small mouth for their weight and are excellent at stealing bait so if this is a species you want to bring back to the house, you will have to go to as small as a size 1/0 hook. In fact, two hooks will produce more action for you. Instead of an egg sinker with a trailing leader attached that holds your hook, tie on a bank sinker. Use a plain loop knot to attach the sinker and it should be as heavy as needed to bounce bottom. In a modest current, fishing from the stern, you should be able to get away with a four to five ounce lead.

Tie two dropper loops into your line, one just above your sinker and the other 18 inches above that. Put two snelled hooks on, with a foot or so of leader. In this manner, your high hook will be off bottom and the lower one will dangle at bottom, giving you the opportunity of catching a double-header.

If you have never tasted the chewy white fillet you get out of a trigger, count on being very pleased because they truly make for excellent eating. A three-inch tapered strip of squid is all you need to catch some of them. Triggers do have a size limit though so make sure you know what it is. Please do note that a very large percentage of the trigger is wasted, from a food standpoint, because of its huge stomach cavity. A one-pounder may only produce four ounces of meat.

#10 MARKER 24 BARGE REEF
Wakulla County

This reef was established in far shallower water than most, so to fish it, you may need to go with lighter gear since the fish tend to be more cautious in shallow water. If you sail 14.2 miles (remember, all our distances are in nautical, not land miles) from St. Marks Lighthouse, you will be in range. The latitude number is 2950.411 and 8409.408 is its longitude location. The reef was built offshore of the St. Marks Wildlife Refuge and not that many miles outside of Apalachee Bay.

If you have the skill as well as a sizeable boat, there is a boat ramp that offers an option to you. It can be found right at Wakulla Beach at the back end of Goose Creek Bay.

The reef was built in 1999 and consists of two major items of structure. A large barge was sunken, along with 387 tons of concrete culverts. Honestly, I don't know if they put both down at the same time or not, but either way, concrete and steel make for a very fine and quite permanent fish farm.

Even in such shallow water, gag grouper are commonly taken

Fish are already visiting these newly added culverts.

here. Try some of that non-stretch line on a heavyweight bait-casting rod and reel. You can handle critters up to 10-20 pounds with that line and its lightweight diameter makes it tough to see for the grouper below you. If you use the more typical boat rod and reel with 40-50 pound mono, you may go without any of your fish of choice so, to repeat, go light here and you may catch a few nice grouper for your effort. Just make sure you know the size limit and even if it looks like a keeper, don't gaff it but carry a serious sized net instead. If it's too small, you can release one that you netted but might cause serious damage with a gaff.

Sea bass are the fish that many seek here because of their wonderful taste. They will not "take drag," but there's little around that can beat the flavor of a sautéed fillet of sea bass. And if you ever go into a Chinese Restaurant and see mostly Chinese customers at the tables, with chop-sticks in hand, you can bet that that whole fish on the table that they are picking at is indeed a sea bass!

Throw in the criminals of the sea (in appearance, anyway),

sheepshead, and you have the threesome, the superb eating three-some, that are at "Marker 24."

#11 STEINHATCHEE REEF
Steinhatchee

The local reef expert for Florida said that there were two sites in his area that stand out. The other one is called the Buckeye Reef, because it consists of 60 tons of pieces of large scrap metal that came from the Buckeye Paper Mill. It is 20.6 miles from Keaton Beach. But let's talk now about one that is closer to shore, the Steinhatchee Reef.

112 huge concrete cubes went down on this site in 1998, only 10.8 nautical miles from Steinhatchee. The concrete sticks up three feet in 20 feet of water, making it pretty close to your boat, so here again, go lightweight for best results.

Travel to latitude 2939.867, longitude 8337.646 to reach this reef, and since it is not that far from shore, if you are confident in your boat handling skills, you may want to run your own boat out to the site. A boat ramp can be found on the south side of Steinhatchee Creek. Take Route 361 across the creek and turn west to the ramp. Go through Deadman Bay until you get to the reef. But please make sure that you have a boat capable of handling sudden storms, especially if there is a forecast for strong winds from the west, which will create severe waves if blowing hard enough.

The Steinhatchee Reef houses a variety of fish, but most sought after are the gag grouper that reside here. Next come sea bass, and after them, sheepshead. While sheepshead are known as fish that prefer hard bait, some will respond to plain old squid. However, if you have access to fiddler crabs, you could find that the biggest sea bass as well as sheepshead will want fiddlers more than any other bait. And as for grouper, if you want to try for them alone, just go to far bigger baits, in particular, live baits. Remember, this is shallow water though. Heavy line could translate into line-shy grouper, so you may have to use that skinny non-stretch stuff here.

#12 CITRUS (CO.) FISH HAVENS (3)
Crystal River

Gag grouper, mangrove (gray) snapper, and triggerfish are out here so let's tell you about these three separate but distinct reefs in close proximity to each other.

Three different sites exist offshore of the Crystal River, but since they are so very close to each other, we will lump them together and give you three locations for the price of one if that's alright with you. First comes the closest one, 20.7 miles out on a southwest direction, to latitude 2847.496, longitude 8303.350. 1300 tons of bridge rubble went down into 30 feet of water, along with a mess of concrete pipes in the spring of 1989. Some of this stuff protrudes upwards as high as 15 feet off the bottom. This place is called Fish Haven, Site A, appropriately enough.

And then, four years later, another 800 tons of concrete rubble was dropped over at latitude 2847.203, longitude 8303.659 into the same 30 foot level, and most of this material is close to the bottom, only four feet or so up. This section is simply called Fish Haven. It's 20.8 miles out.

Last but not least, in 2003, Citrus Fish Haven #1 went down, consisting of 300 concrete poles, into 31 feet of water, 20.7 nautical miles from the river, and some of the poles rise as high as eight feet off bottom. The lat here is 2847.304 with a lon of 8303.497.

Over 20 miles out is a pretty long haul for a private boat, even if it is quite sea worthy so I suggest you try to find a charter boat guy to take you here. But if you have two good engines (one isn't good enough in case it decides to malfunction), and good skills, there are two ramps that are usable for you. One is at the southern tip of the Crystal River, off of Route 44, just before you break out into Crystal Bay, which leads directly into the Gulf. And more to the south, closer, in fact, to the reefs, is a ramp that is at the northwestern tip of Route 494, but if you use this one, you will have to adjust your distance to the reef sites because it will be a somewhat shorter ride.

Take at least two rods for each angler, so that you can "dead-stick" one for grouper and "Grovers" (mangroves), while holding onto a lighter outfit for triggerfish if you want action. Use a two hook rig for triggers, with a bank style sinker to take you down. A size 2/0 or 3/0 hook may be bigger than you need for triggerfish, but if a confused snapper or grouper eats your small bait, you stand a good chance at landing them too. Just make sure your hook is made out of heavy metal, not one of those easy to bend kind. I like Aberdeen or Kahle models for certain fish, but a 10-pound grouper could straighten one of them out so go with a thicker metal.

In particular, on Fish Haven site A, which has stickups as high as 15 feet, you could get hung with ease by a grouper or a snapper so this spot may be best fished with one rod alone, and in your hands at that.

Hire a guide and ask him to try all three separate sections and you may find out that this is one of the best spots in the whole area.

#13 PINE ISLAND
Hernando Beach

Tarpon? For sure, you can catch lots of them down in the Keys, and a bazillion anglers have at these big herring in the vicinity of Charlotte Harbor. But Nancy Forshier of Hernando Beach Bait & Tackle (352-596-3375) said that she feels that more and bigger tarpon are in her area from the start of May until early in July each year. And since she has been in this vicinity for lots of years, who else would know better?

Pine Island is north of Hernando Beach. It lies between Bayport to the north, and Chassahowitzka to the south. And, no, Chassahowitzka is not a town near where my relatives came from in Eastern Europe. It actually is an Indian name for Little Pumpkin, according to Nancy.

The waters of Pine Island literally teem with tarpon in May and June and boats come here from all over to share in the bounty. While redfish and sea trout are in the same water at other times, no one really cares about anything else when the tarpon are in.

The water is only 3-5 feet deep in most of the fishing area so a high-powered boat that charges through may very well get blasted with a heavy sinker or two. Instead, the guys in the know operate their boats with push poles and look for fish to tell their customers to cast to. Blind fishing will produce but since the best action occurs early each morning, and at times, even until noon, once the wind comes up, it is usually all over.

If available, live bait like crabs work very well and many people fish with live shrimp. But the hot shots are often slamming the razor sharp hooks of a Bomber back into the jaw of tarpon hereabouts. A black Bomber, or maybe one with black and silver may be the top plug around. But a close second is a dark green and silver Bomber.

Needless to say, if you are out here in your own boat, please observe the required courtesy and never, not ever, crank your engine up within eyesight of the charter guys. This is suggested in the interest of plain old common courtesy, as well as in the interest of being able to avoid the cusses that would otherwise follow in a heartbeat.

#14 A. H. RICHARDSON REEF (a/k/a "FISH HAVEN")
Hernando Beach

Created in 1989, the above artificial reef wears both of the above names. And to reach it, when she can get away from the store, Ms. Forshier (of Hernando Beach B&T) heads on a 270-degree course out of the Bayport Inlet for 14.7 miles. One of the main chunks is at latitude 2830.50 longitude 8255.80. A buoy labeled "A. H. Richardson" marks a center point of the reef.

The water here is quite shallow, maybe 20 feet or so, and a variety of fish prowl its waters. Among the stuff that has been put down on the reef include the old Sunshine Skyway Bridge material, plus loads of weighted tires, and a gang of bridge culverts.

The water here is comfortable enough most of the year to support a fine number of speckled sea trout. They are known for being more close to shore, but the trout do swim out here and stay a while. Nancy refers to Fish Haven as a "nursery" because so many different species of fish are on it at one time of the year or another.

Come summer, cobia swim on the reef as do a variety of sharks. In the coldest water, black sea bass, the ones that made the swim south from New York and New Jersey and liked it so much that they decided to stay, just like so many other northerners, are on the reef. But the prize sought more than any other fish is usually gag grouper. A variety of grunts are at Fish Haven, and a small one that is hooked near the tail may make your best natural bait around for the grouper. Just be sure to use a heavy fluorocarbon leader to keep the fish from knowing that someone up there wants to hurt him. The reef also houses larger white grunt, some big enough to fillet. The state told me that plenty of mangrove snapper reside on this concrete and metal strewn bottom as well.

Cero mackerel are here every winter, and Spanish mackerel are on the reef much more of the year. A frozen sardine or threadfin, maybe even a ballyhoo, will work for grouper but nothing will beat live bait.

#15 PASCO ONE ARTIFICIAL REEF
Tarpon Springs

Let's credit Captain Rich Knox of *Absolute Flats Fishing* (1-727-376-8809) for giving me most of the information that follows, from here on down to the Boca Grande Pass. And then, while we are at it, let me also tell you that Rich casually mentioned that he won a $280,000 tarpon prize during a contest at The Pass in a recent year!

This superb pile of rubble sits at bottom in 25 feet of water, seven miles from the beach. Sail a 294 heading from the Anclote River to reach the Pasco One. One set of numbers that has lots of stuff under it is at lat 2816.750, lon 8257.450, but as I say often in this book, book a charter or get on a headboat for optimum results.

And what is under the hull of your anchored boat? How about four barges, the hulls of four ships, an old Army tank, and lots of broken up concrete bridge residue.

Springtime means mackerel out here, king and Spanish. There aren't any cero mackerel but since they are far less common throughout Florida, who cares? The bottom holds your typical stuff like grunt and lane snapper, and an occasional mangrove with a few passerby groupers. Most of your fun here will be off bottom on a flat line. A flat line is one that has no sinker, merely your hook set up. But if you are after kings, make sure you are using a double or triple hook, one placed into and out of the eye of the other, in long shank, or have lots of extra hooks to tie on after being chopped off. Kings have a serious set of teeth and many will cut through your single hook's leader quickly. A wire leader is an absolute must if you are going with one hook.

For the Spanish variety, an Ava style jig may produce better than anything. Yes, they have teeth too, but not as much of a problem as their bigger King cuzzins. If there are not any Kings being taken, try to add in a teaser fly above the jig. Flashy mylar on a long shank hook will be all you need if the Spaniards are in town. Double-header catches can be fun but don't take more than you can eat, please.

#16 TARPON SPRINGS REEF
Tarpon Springs

Rich lives in New Port Richey, a bit to the north of The Anclote River where he keeps his boats, and loves to fish a bit to the south further off of Tarpon Springs. And if I was looking to relocate (hint, you Northerners), this may be one of the top areas to check out before heading south. It sure doesn't have the hustle and bustle of the southeast part of the state, but is still close enough to populated areas like Tampa and St. Petersburg to know that plenty of interesting on land attractions exists nearby.

Sailing a course of 282 degrees out of the Anclote will take you to this good-sized area of artificial reef. It rests a little more than seven miles from Tarpon Springs Beach. One of the "numbers" used to find a good stick-up of stone is latitude 2752.864, longitude 8311.077. The closest boat ramp to this reef is well to the north, at Green Key, which is in fact, just about due west of where Rich lives in New Port Richey. So for distance alone, not even considering safety, hire a skipper, please.

Sandperch, members of the grouper family, are on this bottom. And while they may be the very smallest of the clan grouper, they surely are as equally fine eating as their much larger cousins. If you get a ten-incher, it is a biggie, but again, if you want to take a few fish home for a meal, their perfectly white fillets, albeit teenie ones, will please you a great deal. They have a rather large mouth so a size 1 hook on a bottom rig will be okay and such a hook can also hold some of the mangrove snapper that are on station, as well as lanes. Go with a piece of squid or better yet, half of a peeled large dead shrimp.

Here too, as at Pasco One, there often are a good number of mackerel so be certain that your sinker is dull in color. Don't bother painting it black as I have seen some anglers do because that won't work either. The flash of shiny black will attract a King just as quickly as will the brandy new silver lead one will. Rub the sinker on your pants or on a rag to dull it down to help keep it unattractive. You see, the new ones look like a small and tasty niblet to the passing by fish, and they will eat a sinker in a heartbeat.

#17 PASCO TWO
Tarpon Springs

Pasco Two sits about three miles further offshore from Pasco One, on a 294 degree heading out of the Anclote. The water here is 40 feet deep and is, for the most part, an artificial reef. The Tarpon Springs area has benefited greatly from the wonderful program that Florida has for creation of artificial reefs. My guess is that one day, someone (maybe me) will write a book that is ONLY about the artificial reefs in Florida. For now though, this book will feature lots of such reefs but not be solely about them.

Latitude 2817.630 and longitude 8301.090 marks one of the biggest and most productive chunks of this reef and Captain Rich Knox takes his *Double Trouble* out here fairly often.

Here too, the concentration is more on mackerel than anything else. But when a steady wind blows for several days from the west, clouding up the inshore waters, the population of grouper that reside on the inshore wrecks and rocks usually head out to this area. They are seeking water that is easier to see in, and ten miles from the beach, Pasco Two rests 40 feet from the top. This is kind of funny, really, because down around the Keys, the best of the yellowtail snapper activity takes place in cloudy water rather than clear, and the west side grouper want it clearer instead of dirty. Different strokes for different fish, of course.

This reef houses a two hundred foot long barge as well as lots and lots of concrete culverts. Guys who have the necessary skill will pick from both ends of the barge, first anchoring up so that their bait will settle down near the bow, and then lift up and reposition at the stern end. And if fishing was good but it slows down and no one else is around, they may do a third drop, mid-ships, being certain to not stick their anchor deep into the wreck but rather upcurrent so that the bait is presented close to the rubble.

Some call this "The 'Cuda Reef" and you know what that means, I'm sure. It means that you had better reel up your fish very quickly, or else you will need to come up with recipes for cooking fish-head soup, 'cause that's all the 'cuda will leave on your hook.

#18 RUBE ALLYN REEF
Tarpon Springs

Last but far from least of our four chunks of water that are offshore of Tarpon Springs is the well known and popular Rube Allyn Reef. This combination of artificially created reef along with natural coral at bottom makes up a huge expanse of bottom that can fish as many as a dozen boats all at the same time.

The reef sites 17 or so miles from land and a southwest heading of 222 degrees from Anclote gets you to the 44 foot deep waters. And, technically, it's in Pinellas County.

It is usually quite easy to net all the live pilchards you need for bait out here. They are available from mid-February on into December; so most of the year, you have a fine natural supply of bait to present to the beasts below.

And those beasts include lots of black grouper, from throwback size on to ones that will tear up your drag and nail you into the reef in an instant unless you use sturdy enough gear to lift it sufficiently up off bottom.

Chumming with live pilchards can be expensive, unless you

have netted plenty, and you don't want to do this too liberally, just a few at a time, to create a form of feeding frenzy below. During the winter, cigar minnows and sardines are also here but it's tough to net them, so have a rod rigged with a Sabiki set up and catch a dozen or two. Obviously, if you are on a charter boat, a large live bait well will hold all the bait needed.

Two sets of numbers to "Rube Allyn" are lat/lon 2756.127/8301.394 and 2755.749/8301.373.

Come full moon, the best of the mangrove snapper action occurs out here, with plenty of them reaching five pounds. A "Knocker" rig (your egg sinker literally sits on top of your hook's eye instead of via the more traditional long leader) is the way to go. Bait with a live pilchard on this rig for snapper. If grouper are the target species, a 4-5 foot leader below your barrel swivel is preferred. The best time for grouper is in the fall.

Mangroves are the main snappers, but lots of smaller lane are out here too. And from time to time, true red snapper make their presence known.

A chum bag tied off at the bow and another at the stern will produce a good steady pick of fish, especially if you add in some live pilchards into the slick.

All kinds of natural coral plus artificially added wreckage sit here, awaiting your offering. I should add that the State also gave me lots of material about most of the above sites and the distances they use to reach them are somewhat different. And that's because Rich sails from the Anclote and the measurements the state gave me were via Tarpon Springs or Clearwater Pass.

#19 HONEYMOON ISLAND (NORTH END)
North of Dunedin

While Rich loves his tarpon inshore, this spot is his favorite of all for lunker snook. He likes to fish at the north end of Honeymoon Island, at the end of the Dunedin Causeway. The area is within the Honeymoon Island State Park. He has two boats, one that he operates inshore more than the other, but both can sneak into skinny water if need be. His smaller rig is an 18.8 footer with

William McKinnon of Lakeland, Florida caught this 38 inch snook on a live pig fish at Honeymoon Island.

a 175 Mercury kicker. The bigger boat is 24 feet long, and has a tower. Both are called *Double Trouble*. There are many charter boats in this area, as well as quite a few headboats. But you couldn't go wrong if you call him.

Sailing south out of the Anclote River, west of St. Joseph Sound, this area meets the gulf and a good drop-off exists very close to land. If the wind is from the east, you can even fish from shore and cast out to the drop-off. The preferred style is casting from the water towards shore, from west to east. You can't go wrong with a round or torpedo shaped jig in 3/8 to ½ ounce weight. Go with tiger-tail stripe and a silver fleck combination and no, I don't know what kind of small fish that is being duplicated, but the biggest kind of snook like them and that is all that counts.

If you like to use bait, a small grunt may be your best bait of all, the liveliest one you can find. Snook spawn in this area and grunt love to eat snook spawn. Because of that, it is a fact of nature that snook will eat any grunt they can get their mouth around. There are two reasons — to protect their eggs from being gobbled up and to enjoy a hearty meal. Go with a size 2/0 or 3/0 hook, Gamakatsu style. A live pilchard will also produce in this 6-7 foot drop-off. In season or not, please put 'em back. And for sure, do make certain that you have a snook stamp with your license. No, not one that you can mail a letter with, one that Florida sells to you which allows you to fish for snook!

There aren't any ramps nearby, but I suppose a "car-topper" could work, if there is no wind blowing at all and you have a small but trustworthy engine at the ready, if need be.

#20 DUNEDIN REEF
Dunedin

A wide variety of fish are available on this 30 foot deep natural coral reef. It covers upwards of two to three acres of water so can accommodate more than one or two boats with ease. One of the chunks that Captain Knox anchors over wears the latitude number 2805.518 and its longitude is at 8252.525. The heading from his inlet is 292 degrees and the distance is a little over six miles on a southwest course.

If you look in a book that describes one fish from another, they often say that a "gray snapper" is an alias for a "mangrove" snapper. And throughout much of the inner reef areas of the Gulf

Coast, fish are taken that are called "gray snapper," but they sure aren't true snappers. In fact, while no one will confirm this to me, I really think that they are among the larger clan members of the breed GRUNT, by name, white grunt! We used to call these fish "pigfish" but since that isn't as appealing a name as "snapper" is, who cares? By any other name though, they do taste just fine so if you want some "snapper" for a meal, just take a few of them home and tell your better half that you will be eating "gray" snapper, got it?

These fish are found in great number at the Dunedin Reef and will hit just about anything you offer to them. In fact, a fillet, with skin on, from another grunt may be the best bait to use if you want to avoid having it quickly stolen. Squid is probably the top bait used for these pseudo — snappers as well as for regular red-lipped and French grunt on the reef.

There are true mangrove snappers here, to be sure, plus a goodly supply of grouper, black in variety. King and Spanish mackerel round out the critters you will be seeking here.

#21 CLEARWATER REEF
Clearwater

Captain Knox has to take his *Double Trouble* on a further ride to the south to reach this natural coral reef but it really isn't very far for this fast boat. He runs for about eight miles on a southwest heading of 280 degrees to reach the grounds. The reef is really only 4-5 miles from Clearwater Pass. And it contains just about all the other fish you will catch at Dunedin, Pasco One and Two, etc. It merely is another venue that we wanted to tell you about because there are truly so many of them within the same ten-fifteen miles of water.

One of the readings used for the Clearwater Reef is lat 2800.919 and lon 8253.345.

Clearwater may be a place that you would want to take your family to on a vacation. Besides the great fishing that is available offshore, the area offers all kinds of additional goodies to select from. Are you a baseball nut? There are at least three Spring

Training facilities within an hour. And would you like to see fish without stinking your hands up? Try the Clearwater Marine Aquarium off of Route 60. Continue a bit further west and you will find a fine beach and a fishing pier at Clearwater Beach Island. If you want to fly to this area, the Tampa International Airport is nearly a straight shot to Clearwater via Route 60.

#22 BLACKTHORN
Clearwater

What might be the very best of all the bottom structure sites from Tarpon Springs on down to Clearwater is the 180 foot former Coast Guard Cutter called "Blackthorn." It sits in 80 feet of water, quite deep for a mid-coast Gulf location. And it is 19.6 or so miles from Clearwater, with a course of 261 degrees out of the Anclote River for Rich Knox.

The numbers that he sets up over are 2752.570 (lat) and 8311.280 (lon)

More keeper-sized grouper, black and red alike, are caught at Blackthorn than at any other place fished in the immediate area. Well know too are the "Middle Grounds" but again, if your skipper is taking you to Blackthorn, prepare for a fun trip, especially it if hasn't been fished hard during the prior week.

Since you will be in relatively deep water, have a rod with a stiff, non-forgiving tip that won't bend over double after you stick the hook. If the rod is "fast-action," the whippiness of it will bend the rod too much and allow the grouper to take enough line to get you stuck in one of its many favorite hunks of rock. At such times, don't just pull and cut yourself off. I have often been lucky enough to have my fish get tired of hiding, and since the line is slack, it may just swim back out of the hole. If you sense an ever so slight movement, you may just have a fish in open water, ready to be reeled up. I caught a 21-pound black that way once and had to wait it out for fully five minutes before it came out and let me know it was there for the retrieving.

For grouper, use an egg sinker that will take you to the bottom with no slack. Stop it with a dark barrel swivel and tie a five foot length of line, maybe fluorocarbon line if you believe in that stuff, but better yet, some non-stretch stuff. To the end of that line, tie on a size 6/0 or even a 7/0 stiff wire hook. Your bait could be a dead sardine or maybe a live bait if available, like a small grunt. But you may do well also if you use a chunk cut out of a recently caught Spanish mackerel. Grouper want something worth eating, so if in doubt, go bigger rather than smaller. You know that "big bait means big fish," right?

#23 THE SHERIDAN
Clearwater

There were two very separate and distinct sinkings out off of Clearwater in the '80's. Four years after the prior vessel (the Blackthorn) was sunk, the State put the 180 foot former tug boat, Sheridan, down quite close by. The state refers to them as Pinellas II — Sheridan (W), and Pinellas II — Blackthorn.

Mangrove snapper are the main attraction here. Next come gag grouper, and taking up the rear are the ever-present sheepshead. The latter fish is not all that common this far out to sea but the guys at the state said there are plenty of them on both wrecks.

The Sheridan is only 1/10 of a mile closer to the beach than the Blackthorn, 19.5 nautical miles out. The numbers are 2752.562, 8311.180. The depth here is also 80 feet and some of the metal sticks as high up off bottom as 30 feet. In such areas, amberjack are always a possibility. They like to be off bottom but the high stack may be where you find a few of them, picking off unsuspecting bait-fish.

Have you ever fished a "plug?" By any name, this style of fresh cut hunk of bait may be the very best offering you can present to both mangrove snapper and grouper. And the best thing about it is that it is virtually indestructible. You can keep a "plug" on forever, if you want to wait out a big fish bite.

And how can you create such a fine offering? Take any small fresh caught fish that has no size or bag limit, and prepare it for the dining table that waits below you. Since grunt are the usual vic-tims, and because they are just about everywhere, let's catch a few and keep them alive. But instead of using whole and lively bait, try a "plug." We will talk about this bait several times during the book, for good reason... it works great!

First of all, cut the head and tail off. Now that the fish has stopped wiggling, then use a good heavy and sharp pair of scissors, and remove all of the fins from around the entire perimeter of the remaining fish. Some guys take their knife and do the same thing, cutting away all of the fins and exposing a little bit of flesh at the same time. In fact, this is the best way to set up a plug for that very reason. But if the boat is rocking and your knife isn't all that sharp, go second best and use the scissors.

And now you have a "plug." Stick a size 6/0 hook into the tail end of the chunk and run it completely through. No, don't bury it, please. Drop the bait to the bottom and reel up a few feet, with a long leader, and wait for a big, big bite. Forget about the little guys that may bother your bait. Your bait is too big for them and you are after larger fish anyway, right? You may not get more than one bite every half-hour that you can respond to, but when you do, it will probably be something that was worth the nearly 20 mile ride to the wrecks. A "grover" that eats a plug will virtually always be well over 3 or 4 pounds, and most grouper too should be at or over the legal size limit. Enjoy, and don't take too many home.

#24 THE SEVENTY FATHOM PEAKS
Offshore of Bradenton

Let's see, a fathom equals six feet so 70 x 6? Wow, there's a 420 foot drop to the bottom nearby, but the "Peaks" climb up to as close as 65 feet to the surface. There are six peaks in this area that jut well up on a slope above the bottom, and around these peaks is where Captain Bill White (941-351-7135) of the *Eagle Ray* fishes as often as he can. Leaving his slip at Long Boat Pass in Bradenton, skipper White heads on a compass reading of 220 degrees to reach some of his favorite projections. This is 98 miles from momma, so for sure, don't you dare try it yourself.

Summer time, in particular, is when to charter a boat for a trip to the Peaks, and mid-June is the very best time of the year (the

Want tuna in the Gulf – try here!

hotter, the better).

Just about every kind of big critter can be caught in these waters. With the surrounding water so very deep, small fish hide around the outcroppings, and bigger fish come to feed.

There are two basic styles of fishing: live-lining large bait fish or trolling. Trolling is done off of outriggers or planer boards. Captain Bill pulls eight inch Bombers in mullet finish, and also likes to use a 20-inch skirt in pink or green. The action usually centers around the depths of 10 to 30 feet below the surface.

Want big amberjacks? "A-J"s to 80 pounds are common. Tuna, including yellowfin, big eye and blackfin, are probably caught in larger numbers than anything else here. But dolphin are also present, as are wahoo, sails, and marlin.

This is never-never land for topwater anglers who like to catch big fish while sitting in a chair. Of course when someone hands you the rod though, you had better be ready for a beast that may be unlike anything you ever hooked before. Or else get someone stronger than you to crank the handle.

#25 THE MIDDLE GROUNDS
Offshore of Bradenton

As we move further into the book, you will see that my favorite place is the Dry Tortugas. But honestly, that may be because I never fished the fabled "Middle Grounds!" From what I've heard and been told, if you want grouper and snapper, you may find that this area is the very best in the whole state of Florida to fish.

Captain White told me that Florida doesn't allow any kind of commercial fishing out here at all, nothing, nada, zilch, got it? That means no long liners, draggers, and he even said that charter dive guys cannot come here to stick fish for sale. Add to the mix the simple fact that only true experienced boaters dare go here, so you know that the Middle Grounds does not get the pressure that other waters get. Simply put, you don't dare try it yourself as it is simply too darn far for a private boat, period!

The 40' *Eagle Ray* leaves Long Boat Pass inlet and takes a 280 degree heading until it reaches the closest part of the grounds. And that's 104 miles from land. This, the east end comes first, and then the middle of the Middle, and lastly, 140 miles away, comes the west end, which bites down into the deeper waters of the Continental Shelf.

The Middle Grounds covers 240 square miles, and consists of ancient coral reefs and ledges that form a wonderful natural feeding and breeding ground for every kind of large bottom dweller available.

Want grouper? It offers black and red grouper. And gag and scamp. Also speckled hind and snowy. Now try snapper — true red snapper are here along with their baby look-alikes, vermilion. The "red" is easy to tell apart from a vermilion if you have both on deck, forgetting about size. But to confuse things, they also have Queen

A 22 and 19 pound grouper caught on the Middle Grounds.

snapper, which look like a vermilion with extra long tail tips. Dogtooth snapper are on the Grounds as are mangrove and in the summer, some muttons.

Since hooks and lines are so uncommon, the fish aren't as shy as elsewhere. Instead of a long leader, all that Bill uses on his rods is an eight ounce egg sinker, stopped by a barrel swivel, and only an 18 inch 60 pound leader. The hook is a 7/0 circle. Bait can be dead or alive... the fish aren't that particular where no one is otherwise pestering them.

Who knows, so much water and so little time. I may find time though to get out here, I hope, I hope, I hope.

#26 MIDDLE GROUND (FLAT!)
Inside of Sarasota Bay

And for sure, this "Middle Grounds" is far, far closer to land than the one we just discussed. In fact, these grounds are within easy sight of downtown Sarasota, but even though being so close to civilization, the waters are remarkably clear. Captain Rick Grassett runs *Snook Fin-Addict Guide Service* (1-941-923-7799) and takes his 18-foot flats boat into the bay very often in search of fish, and usually connects.

The Middle Grounds Flats are just inside of New Pass on the north side of the bay. Nearby is the "Radio Tower" Flat which is on the south side, and both are formed by deep grass flats, from 4-6 feet deep.

Sea trout make up a large portion of the fish that Captain Rick's customers catch. He uses a D. O. A. Cal jig in gold or silver for best results. But in overcast days, he goes with a darker color, maybe root beer. He likes plastic baits of all kinds to use on spinning gear with a small jig often being the best to use.

Pompano are present in the flats, along with bluefish in the winter.

The bay is protected well from most winds even though it is three miles wide and 10 miles long at its maximums. Southeast and northwest blows in high velocity are the two directions that bother him the most.

There are two boat ramps that can bring you here. Check out location M-1, two waters from now, for directions to these convenient spots. By the way, there are several good swimming beaches in this area. Try the one at Lido Beach and for better swimmers, South Lido Beach may be more fun. Make sure you obey the warnings though, especially on a stiff wind from the west.

#27 POINT OF ROCKS
Sarasota

This location is in the Gulf, at the southern part of Siesta Key. Long Boat Pass is to the north and New Pass and Big Sarasota Pass are down to the south a bit.

Captain Rick follows a south by southeast direction when he leaves Sarasota Bay as he heads down to the Point of Rocks. This is natural hard bottom and it extends 5-6 miles out to Grassy Point. The area he fishes starts as close in as 100-200 yards off the beach and is 15 feet deep that close in. As it slopes westward, the productive water becomes 30 feet deep ½ mile from the beach.

Rick likes to look for crab trap floats in these waters. Carefully and quietly sneaking up on them, he looks for black shadows. And these will almost look like plastic bags but instead will be tripletails that lie on their side, hiding and waiting for a passerby baitfish. At times, a far larger shadow will be present in the form of a cobia.

At such times, a gentle presentation of a lure is critically important because you don't want to scare the fish. Rick really loves to put his customers into fish via the light wand, but fly or lure, stealthlike movement is important.

Rick ties his own flies in olive or brown on a size one or two Mustad #34007 stainless steel hook. A slow-sinking fly is best and the hook shank is bent back so that the fly rides hook up in the water. A D. O. A. shrimp lure is a great second choice.

The top time for tripletails is spring and fall. Since cobia are much larger, a bigger fly, like a deceiver, is generally used at the crab trap floats when such fish are present. Bigger fish will also hit a jerk worm rigged on a ¼ ounce jig head, cast via a spinning rod. Just remember to have a smooth running drag because some of these critters can smoke line off your reel.

For Spanish mackerel, the Point of Rocks area fishing involves the use of a fly on a long shank size 1 hook in beak style. His favorite colors are white or white and tan. A flash of mylar couldn't hurt either. An alternate for flash would be to tie on some "Ultra-hair."

Tripletail, cobia, and Spanish mackerel. That makes for quite an interesting combination and all in the same general area. How bad could it be?

#28 "M-1"
Sarasota

Let's head out offshore a bit now, to the artificial reef that wears the name "M-1." And to reach the stuff that awaits you, travel 6.9 miles out from New Pass. If you are in your own boat, you can launch at two convenient locations in Sarasota Bay. One is just west of route 41/45, and near the Municipal Pier (which may be worth a visit). And the other is even closer to the inlet, at Radio Towers. You will be close to the Mote Marine Aquarium, which could be worth a visit for the little ones.

You should head out to latitude 2719.172, longitude 8243.164, to get to the place that was created in 1993 by the dropping of a load of concrete catch basins along with 733 tons of concrete culverts. Needless to say, the unbroken material is hollow and offers an incredible number of places for fish to take up residence in. You can count on grouper, in particular, that have spent most of their lives out here. They know the way to take you into one opening and out another so quickly that your mouth might drop open when it hangs you up. But such are the woes that face a grouper angler.

The water here is 42 feet deep and material rises up only five feet or so, meaning that most of it is parallel to the bottom.

White grunt are the main victims that attract bigger fish to the dining table at M-1. But white grunt themselves can and often do reach filleting size, and make for good eating. I caught a two pounder off of Palm Beach one day and my neighbor told me that it provided a fine meal.

But if you catch some smaller grunt, try a live one for bait. Far and away though, the best baitfish are pinfish out here, but they aren't easy to catch. If you have a livewell available, buy a few dozen and use them for the mangrove snapper and gag grouper at M-1.

Some anglers like to remove part of the top fin of a pinfish to make it swim even more aggressively so that it attracts predators even more. (As an aside, your squeamish son or daughter may not want to witness this so leave them at the Aquarium, maybe).

#29 VENICE INLET
Venice

According to Frank Sargeant, a true pro on the water and at his computer, the area from Tampa Bay on down to Marco Island holds loads of tarpon from early in May to the middle of July. But other than, perhaps, Boca Grande Pass, at the mouth of Charlotte Harbor, the outer side of Venice Inlet holds as many tarpon as anywhere else. And the beauty of it is that it isn't fished nearly as hard!

My copy of the 2003 DeLorme Atlas didn't show it, but Frank said that there is a public boat ramp just inside and south of the inlet, something important to know. Fishing in this area usually involves bait and the bait of choice is a live blueclaw crab. Plugs work as well but tarpon feed aggressively on live bait early each morning very close to the beach.

Use of such hard bait requires the fisherman to put a stiff action rod into play with a razor sharp size 7/0 hook tied at the business end. Don't try to hook a tarpon with a little sissy set. No indeed, a short but fast slam to the sky is required, followed maybe by one or two more sets to make sure the hook got into the hard jaw of the fish.

The area a bit offshore of North Jetty Park is a fine place to start off. Try just electric motor riding to avoid scaring off fish as you seek them out. Their silvery sides will flash in the early sun and then all you need do is stop your knees from knocking long enough to allow you to cast ahead of the fish.

Tarpon swim parallel to the beach in water depths of 10-25 feet, anywhere from 200-500 yards from the sand.

Venice Beach is found to the south of the inlet and nearby is a nice fishing pier. Don't expect to see any of the kinds of attractions found clear across the country in Venice Beach, California though. This area is vastly different in every way possible.

A wide variety of other fish are available inside of Venice Inlet. They include sea trout, redfish (channel bass) and snook. Try the early morning outside for tarpon and then head back into Donna or Roberts Bay to cast for these three other game fish. Have a much lighter rod at the ready to fish for them. Try either live shrimp or a plastic tout.

#30 GASPARILLA PASS/SOUND
Placida

The Pass is gone through from the Gulf to reach Placida Harbor to the north or Gasparilla Sound to the south. Placida Harbor houses more snook than anything, followed by redfish and trout. Most of this area is in Charlotte County, well to the north of Boca Grande in Lee County. The good people at Mercury Motors have a test center in the back of the Harbor so put an ear plug or two in when they are chasing around, testing their new engines, to avoid a headache.

A fine boat ramp is located on the Placida Harbor side of Route 771 (Gasparilla Causeway) which crosses over from Placida to Big Gasparilla Island. This is a small but popular site though, so arrive very early on a weekday or expect to have trouble parking. Little Gasparilla Island is on the north side of the pass. And if all this is confusing, not to worry. All you need know is that the pass itself as well as the Harbor and Sound are fine waters to fish. There are at least three other launch sites (pay) near Eldred's, or at Gasparilla Marine, or the one on Gasparilla Island itself.

Stick to the outer edges of the Mercury facility if you want to avoid getting yelled at but still be in range of lots of trout, snook or redfish because the motor power attracts bait which, in turn, attract fish to feed on them. The largest number of sea trout are caught here in the winter.

Nearby is Gasparilla Marine which has a nice 7 — foot channel

This fine redfish ate Frank Sargeant's plug.

that runs into Catfish Creek. Again, trout are number one but some fine snook will appear as well. The best time for this action is late November through the month of December. Sargeant suggests bouncing a 1/¼ ounce jig on bottom for the trout but a noisy topwater plug for snook.

You are not going to find much deep water anywhere in this area and if you have the back for it, a push pole could bring results when you aren't competing against the wave wash from Mercury kickers.

#31 PHOSPHATE DOCKS
Gasparilla Island (southern end)

Gasparilla Island runs in a southerly direction from Gasparilla Pass way on down to Boca Grande where we will soon find gigantic schools of tarpon playing just outside. But we will get to that later. For now, let's fish inside of Charlotte Harbor in an area that is best known for its large population of beast-length snook.

As with most other snook spots, this one is best fished in the dark of night. Frank said that a ratio of 100-1 is the norm so forget daylight and get ready to miss some sleep. It will be well worth the yawns. He feels that more 20+ pounders reside nearby than anywhere else along the entire gulf coast.

The docks run out into 32 feet of water and the water is loaded with every kind of lure grabbing structure imaginable from busted pilings to cables and the like.

If, somehow or another, you have managed to get permission to fish from the docks, you still will need monster-strength tackle. Did you ever see the old films of commercial tuna fishermen at sea, standing in a pile of stacked up fish? Well, those guys used extra heavy calcutta/bamboo poles with ridiculously heavy breaking strength line and when a tuna bit, they would lift with all their might and sling their catch into the mass of slithering fish.

A variation of this works from the pier but it's not for the weak of muscle or back, and certainly is not for game fishermen anywhere. A similar pole is put into play with one pound sash-weights that hold huge shrimp in place in the fast current below. Some guys would also use a half-pound ladyfish as bait but the style remains drop and horse 'em in.

Boat fishermen will need light to see by, and still, plenty heavy tackle to try to keep from breaking up in the snags that Mr. Snook will carry you into otherwise. Anchor your boat uptide of the pilings on outgoing tide and present your bait (live pinfish or sardine if you can get them) as close to the wood as you dare. You will need a heavy Danforth anchor with chain and lots of 3/8 inch nylon anchor line. Be careful to watch that you won't get too close to the dock because the closer you get, the more the likelihood of a hooked fish playing ring around the wood with you.

Come late summer, heavyweight redfish are in the area and fun to catch and put back. Again, go heavy in the fast water with a ½ or full ounce jig bounced on bottom. You can also do business if you can get a live bait down to the bottom.

We will meet up again soon with Frank Sergeant, but for now, let's hear from someone else. Don't forget though to pick up one or more of Frank's books, which we will talk about at greater length after talking about Rookery Bay down Marco Island way, okay?

#32 BOCA GRANDE PASS
Charlotte Harbor

The mouth of Charlotte Harbor wears this name and while fish do pass through it often, thousands of tarpon stop long enough to feed every spring. Captain Ralph Allen (1-941-639-2628) adds to his living nicely by guiding anglers to the Pass.

Captain Allen has a small fleet of boats, several for the white clothing brigade (sightseeing boats), three that fish the back-bays, and two charter boats as well. Ralph feels that the spring tarpon run in the mouth of Charlotte Harbor is the best one in the whole world.

Starting late in April and continuing until early July, his boats are out on a daily basis with experienced as well as novice anglers all enjoying themselves. As summer moves forward, he finds tarpon still in the inner waterways, clear up to and sometimes through September. For now though, let's try a day in June.

Drifting is the style in the name of sanity and self-protection. One doesn't want to anchor up in the path of what could be hundreds of drifting boats, nosirree, one doesn't indeed.

Captain Allen fishes two basic styles: live bait and jigging. For live bait, he likes sand perch or squirrel fish. By night the bait of choice becomes live crab or the biggest live shrimp you can buy. Free-line your bait by day but hold it down at night with a sinker.

Tarpon feed in the pass on moving water better than at slack. As it slackens, you can improve your catch by jigging. Captain Allen uses a red and dark green model for top results.

Good eating mangrove snapper often are taken in the Pass each summer. Go smaller and lighter for optimum results. Live shrimp may be best but a strip of squid can even do it.

"Catch and release" your tarpon, please. A mount is a pretty sight, but you can take measurements and a reproduction can be on your wall that will be a virtual duplicate.

#33 BOCA GRANDE BAR
Offshore of Charlotte Harbor

Skipper Ralph Allen of the *Kingfisher* and *Kingfisher II* likes to fish this huge shoal of water from springtime to autumn. A wide variety of shiny critters chug through the shallow waters of the Bar and it covers three miles so you need not fish in a crowd.

The Bar starts only a few hundred yards out from Charlotte Harbor and ranges out for a few miles. It runs from the northeast to the southwest and on low water, some sections are as shallow as five feet deep.

Spanish mackerel are the main target species but ladyfish, blue runners, jack crevalle and even some bluefish are taken on the Bar. Trolling is the main style but some guys like to anchor up and chum, fishing bait for the inhabitants below. This often produces some wild action as a huge barracuda may suddenly appear and eat all your fish off the hooks for an hour or two. So be warned, chum and catch fish, but a mouthful of teeth may require you to re-rig and re-rig and re-rig again.

Trolling a Clark squid spoon works well on the Spanish mackerel. A jig will do it too and if you have access to any of the old Tony Accetta spoons, go with them. They have a nice shape and a touch of red to help attract your fish. I have done well with a metal jig and a couple of red teasers tied in above. If any of you are from the northland (the two "New's in particular, Jersey and York), you will remember fishing for "Boston" mackerel with this kind of teaser. If you can find some, or have a buddy that can mail you a few from those areas, try them. You may find that your Spanish catches are as good as your "Boston" catches were and for sure, you will be lots warmer too. And the Spanish taste better anyway.

For the prior location, Boca Grande Pass, and the Bar, your closest boat ramps can be found at Placida and Pine Island. Enjoy both sites, please.

#34 CHARLIE'S REEF
Boca Grande

Two separate piles of hopper cars were barged out to this site, 26.2 miles out from Boca Grande, back in 1994. In total, 40 cars in all were sunken and that makes for quite a load of metal sitting down at bottom, attracting life. Two kinds of snapper inhabit the steel, and each is a fine food fish, but in truth, one likes to eat the other as much as you might like to eat both of them.

Mangrove snapper are the fish that most anglers seek at "Charlie's," followed by their much smaller far removed kissin' cuzzins, lanes. A lane snapper is very small in comparison to mangroves, but some do reach three or four pounds. But since the size limit, at least when I wrote this book, was only eight inches for a lane, you need to know that they aren't all that big.

Since you will be far from the beach, I hope you will be at Charlie's via a charter boat. Therefore, before doing the following, make sure to ask the skipper if it's legal or not. Again, if legal only, take your first small legal-sized lane and use it for bait. Presuming it is allowed, you will still have to count the fish in your overall snapper bag limit so be sure you can do this, and make sure to keep an accurate count.

And if it is okay, that eight or nine inch lane could hook you up with one of the biggest mangroves that you ever caught because mangroves have no respect for family at all. They will just as soon eat a small lane as they would a live pinfish. By the way, there are some gag grouper at the hopper cars so they may also like to feed on your bait.

Goliath grouper and friends on Charlie's Reef.

Presuming, though, that you are after lanes for the table, there are a few ways to catch them in good number. Far and away my best catches of lane snapper have come from using a two hook rig with fresh strips of grunt as bait. I caught one back in the 90's that went 3½ pounds on such a bait.

Fillet a few fresh grunt, carefully cutting away all of the back bones, and then cut the meat into strips from back down to belly. You will have strips of meat that, with skin on, will stay on the hook quite well but still be easy to ingest for the smaller mouthed lanes.

I know that most guys cut hunks as bait but in my own personal experience, I really prefer to use the fluttering fillet, especially cut the way just noted. In this manner, you will offer a strip that has varied colors to add to the appeal. If you use two hooks, try putting one through the lighter color and skinnier belly part. And then place hook number two through the thicker back part of your second strip. Try to note which one gets hit more and then switch over to use both strips the same way. Just hook the bait once, don't wind it in and out-let it flutter, that is key. And if a mangrove eats your strip, there's no law you cannot keep it in with your lanes, providing you obey the overall bag limit in force at the time you are out there.

The cars stand way up from bottom and the center lat point is 2633.373 with a lon of 8243.367.

#35 EDISON REEF
Sanibel/Fort Myers Beach

This reef is well within range of the faster half-day boats out of Fort Myers Beach. The state gave me a measurement from the Sanibel Lighthouse and it's only 14.2 miles south by southwest from the light. Captain Francis Hutson of the *Lady Renee* (239-267-6884) told me that he takes a heading of 240 degrees from the *Gettaway* Dock and sails 14½ miles to reach this site. Francis said that this spot is called "The Edison Reef" because it consists of material that had been part of the original Edison Bridge. The numbers needed will be latitude 2618.541, longitude 8213.250.

You will be fishing in 45 feet of water and the reef stands well up in the water from bottom, maybe as high as 16 feet in places. This reef consists of concrete bridge spans and as noted, some slabs aren't flat to the bottom, therefore the stickup height noted.

The Edison Reef was created in 1993 and the most commonly caught snapper out here is the ever-present mangrove (gray). The state feels that the second most commonly found fish on this reef are sheepshead and a good number of gag grouper also call it home.

For sheepshead, you need to respond far quicker than you do for snapper and grouper. In fact, if you try to stick the two other fish as fast, you will miss more than you catch so try to fish two entirely different methods here.

If you can find some, sand fleas on small hooks produce wonderful results for sheepshead. And if you are lucky enough to have a tackle store near you that carries fiddler crabs, they make a fine second best.

Northern anglers may have a slight advantage now, but even if you never heard of this hook, you should be able to find some, somewhere, a hook that I like for sheepshead. It is made by Mustad and the style is called "Virginia." The model number is 4011E. Different in measurement from most hooks, my size of choice is a size 4. And this particular hook in "4" is much bigger than most other traditional hooks so don't think I'm touting you onto too small a hook.

The hook is blue in color and has a weird bend to it. The bend allows you to stick the hook into one claw opening of a fiddler and out the other, with ease. And the bend itself will hold the bait onto your hook much better than any other hook will. The fish that this hook is most commonly used for is called "Tautog," blackfish, or slippery bass up north, but this hook will work equally well on sheepshead and it is strong enough, even in a smaller size, to catch snapper and grouper on.

#36 BIG LEDGE
Fort Myers Beach

Considered by Captain Hutson to be "the hardest fished" chunk in the whole area, he nevertheless fishes out here from time to time. And having been in this section of Florida for well more than 30 years, he not only knows it, but at which angles to set up anchor over to be on the most productive sections.

The Big Ledge covers upwards of 500 yards of bottom, and it runs in a north to south direction. But to position the boat over some of the five to six foot breaks in the bottom, he likes to approach it from north-west to south-east before sticking the anchor in. A variation of 65-72 feet of water is present due to the breaks in the hard rock bottom below. Running south by southwest on a course of 240 degrees, he reaches a main section of the ledge at lat 2613.001, lon 8222.781.

Hogfish, sometimes called "Hog snapper," even though they aren't a snapper at all, are often caught out here. And since they may be among the very best tasting fish in the entire state of Florida, let's try for a few. By the way, they are a member of the Wrasse family if you care to know it.

They have a serious set of teeth and their diet consists of hard food. With their choppers, they have an easy time of getting and taking care of anything, other than, maybe, a hard clam. A large and lively shrimp would be number one. Small lobsters are often found in their bellies. And crabs make up the majority of what they eat. I caught one out of Fort Lauderdale one day on, of all things, a fillet of sardine, but again, try hard bait. The main problem with using live shrimp for hogfish is that the other fish on The Big Ledge have no respect for privacy. While you may be after a hog, everything else will try to snatch your bait away. So if you don't have a lot of money or maybe a private source for an unlimited supply of large and live shrimp, go for the other critters out here.

One such critter is king mackerel and they are on station when the water temperature is around 72 degrees. This generally occurs in late winter through early spring. Spanish mackerel swim through often and might take your king offering. Since kings have a size limit, if you want to take some mackerel home, the easiest way to tell the difference is that kings have little added coloration to their silver-blue bodies but Spanish (and cero) mackerel each have yellow spots all over the place.

Mangrove snapper are here, along with some black grouper, mostly undersized ones, and for those who want action, go with smaller hooks and bait for triggerfish, grunt and lane snapper.

#37 STONY POINT
Fort Myers Beach

Way back in the early 70's, maybe even a few years earlier, this big old ferry boat took its last ride into the gulf to be intentionally sunk, creating an artificial reef. My guess is that accurate records exist that will say who the team of farsighted anglers were who arranged for this event, but instead of focusing on whodunit, let's instead take advantage of the good that they done!

Although resting in the sand for so many years, Captain Francis Hutson told me that the vessel remains quite intact and presents a fine profile, clearly showing its full length on his sonar equipment. And as he searches the wreck to determine which angle to first anchor up over, he often sees a pile of fish well off bottom.

Regardless of who he is and how often he sees suspended fish, this can really get his juices flowing. Be they tuna or pollock way to the north, or amberjack or cobia down south, a reading of fish well above the wreckage nearly always insures a successful trip for his customers.

Even before anchoring up, Francis has the mate have a few rods rigged with jigs. Instead of pure chrome ones, he prefers a green colored model and adds to the attraction with a large trout tout on his 8/0 hooks. The plastic attachment can either be green or fluorescent white.

Using a 4-6 ounce jig, depending on current, he has his fares drop 2/3 of the way down to the bottom and retrieve upwards, jerking up and down all the way. Many of the times, the jig will be stopped on its downward drop and you may think that your jig was chopped off due to the fact that your line went slack. This requires instant attention because a fish has slammed and swum upward.

This one is really way too far out for nearly all private boaters, but for the record, the latitude is 2610.335 and the longitude is 8254.530, but please don't try it alone. The wreck sits in 140 feet of water, 55 miles from the Miss Renee's dock, and at times, they will fish it at night. Nighttime translates into cobia time, and some anglers swear that they prefer this "ling" to most other fish in the Gulf. Winter is the best time to fish the Stony Point because that is when the top action occurs from cobia.

Amberjack are nearly always present, and if you don't want to jig for them, use of a live bait, slowly dropped down, will often result in a slam anywhere from 35-45 feet below the surface. Of course "A-J's" swim anywhere they want, but this is a good depth to try.

There aren't many grouper on the Stony Point but some of the best mangrove fishing he has access to in these waters can be found at this wreck. And in the winter, a swarm of yellowtail snapper often visit. Since there really aren't that many sections of the Gulf that house yellowtails, you should take notice of this. A winter charter could produce a fine variety of great eating fish. Yellowtails at bottom and cobia half-way down. Not bad!

#38 NORTHWEST BOTTOM
Naples

Sail 283 degrees out of Gordon Pass for 13.8 to 13.9 miles and you will reach a vast area of hard bottom that is commonly called "Northwest Bottom" by the local headboat and charter boat guys. Its main GPS numbers are 2608.464/8203.947 and 2608.580/8156.369.

Captain Gene Luciano of the 45-foot headboat, *Lady Brett* (239-263-4949) fishes here often, the year 'round, and does things a bit differently from many of the other boats that fish here. Most boats stick to squid or cut up pieces of the grunt and other small fish they catch as bait. Gene feels that his customers can produce a better quality catch by using more expensive bait, frozen threadfin. His mates cut the bait into two or three pieces and a somewhat larger hook is used than the more typical size 1 or 1/0. Instead of seeking grunt and spottails, he is trying to put his fares into lane and mangrove snapper.

The best of the mangrove action occurs each winter. Common visitors also include red and gag grouper. Most are under the size limit but a keeper is something that is always waiting right near the next pothole at bottom.

The rig includes a single 3/0 or 4/0 heavy wire hook on a leader tied below a barrel swivel which has a three or four ounce egg sinker sitting on top of it. For the most part, they anchor up once fish are found on the scope, but Capt. Luciano uses a unique approach at marking his selected chunk before he anchors up. Checking wind and current, he marks the bottom with a very light weight floating dinner plate and tries to shut of the engines with the plate popping up and down on top, dead behind the stern.

Kingfish are generally caught best in October and November when the water temperature averages 74-76 degrees, but some are usually on station most of the year. And if the boat isn't loaded with customers, he may also slowly drag baitfish from the rear for kings. Bonito, those wonderful fighting but very strong tasting critters, are always around the boat. You can tell that you've hooked one when your drag screams out in protest. And then as you get it close

I caught this 8 pound kingfish while flatlining.

to the boat, that tell-tale thumpety-thump of the rod tip separates it from nearly all other fish.

#39 SOUTHWEST BOTTOM
Naples

Generally better in the summer, the *Lady Brett* fishes here at other times also. Red grouper are the primary target on this vast expanse of hard bottom, even though most are under the size limit. But in the winter, when the current is very light, a rather different style of fishing is used, and the critter sought is mangrove snapper. This spot is reached at 2559.893/8159.684, 11 miles from Naples on a 236 degree heading.

At such times, it is far better to fish off the stern, unless a sideways current is present. Mangroves are commonly brought up high in the water column by lightly chumming with ground baitfish as well as small chunks of them. And the rig is nowhere similar to the weighted one used most of the time. This style is called "Flatlining," and we do it often for dolphin and kingfish, but try it for snapper when conditions favor the style.

Again, when the tide is modest, ditto the wind, a single hook is stuck through the eyes of a threadfin and allowed to flop out in the current. No sinker, period, is in use. If you have a heavy spinning rod and reel combo, cast the offering out underhand. The bait sinks ever so slowly and Mr. Mangrove is down there, attracted by chum, waiting to bite. You can generally tell the bite of a mangrove. It's kind of like a freight train careening out of control. Keep the reel open and let it streak away five or ten feet, close the reel and stick the tip skyward and if you did it right, you hooked a fine fish. Of course if you did it wrong you got one super backlash, but that's something you may get cured of some day.

#40 EMPRESS HONDURAS AND OILER WRECKS
Naples

These sites are not for the Sunday Sailors, to be sure. Captain Luciano of the *Lady Brett* told me that he has dove on both wrecks and has seen some really outsized specimens on them, but again, forget about it and stick to the charter or headboats that can reach them.

The 200+ feet Empress Honduras has jeeps on board that add to the attraction for true black and gag grouper. Captain Luciano dove it a series of times and successfully removed a fourteen square foot propeller, so you know this is a big vessel that sunk years ago. Follow a heading of 210 degrees out of Gordon Pass and you will have to sail 55+ miles out before it can be reached. The ship sits in about 110 feet of water so make sure you use a stiff rod to haul up or else the grouper will nail your sinker to the steering wheel of one of its favorite jeeps. This vessel is found via his Loran at 13920.7/43961.8.

And still further out, a full 70 miles from the inlet, is the "Oiler," a ship that doesn't have a visible name. The Loran numbers are 13851.0/44008.8. It's called this because after many years, it still leaks oil. The 400-footer sites on its side in 140 feet of water. The Empress Honduras that we just discussed houses lots of grouper, as does the Oiler. But more fish sit higher in the water column out here than at the Empress. You can find a gang of marauding barracuda often on this wreck, up high. And then some amberjack will be halfway down, Permit join with them in the spring and summer, and African pompano travel on this wreckage also.

While mangrove snapper are present, their bigger and some-what lookalike cousins, Cubera snappers, are also on the Oiler. They grow big and nasty here.

Never venture out to either wreck unless you have a Captain's license and two good fast engines. Of course your boat should be quite seaworthy because, urph, the seas can mount to extreme heights this far out to sea.

And as a further bonus, let's add in another wreck, called Spot Peck, found at 13838.5/44011.9. Remember, get to these places on a charter boat, they are too far out for non-professionals to dream of sailing to.

#41 GORDON PASS
Naples

Remember the old "Green Grass Syndrome?" Oh, you know, "the grass is greener on the other side of the fence" is how it goes. Well, we just talked about a bunch of locations that are reached by sailing out of Gordon Pass in Naples, but now, let's stay inside the pass, which is a bit to the south of yet another site you may want to visit, the excellent Naples Municipal Pier.

So, courtesy of Frank Sargeant, let's talk about the fine fishery that is available to small boaters before you even have to venture out into the gulf. Gordon Pass is what the boats go out of from Naples Bay. The Bay is created by the outfall of Gordon River, Rock Creek and Haldeman Creek. If you check out the Atlas, you will see that the southern end of Naples is literally crawling with all kinds of canals that remind me of a Disney (or airport security) waiting line. I won a prize in a Cortland Tackle lying contest many years ago involving a whopper I made up regarding the similar waters of the Mullica River in South Jersey, but that's a story for another day altogether.

Many of the cuts that jut in and out can and often do hold some impressive snook. But those that are closest to the larger canals near Gordon Pass are tops. These cuts run from 10-14 feet deep and are far wider than the skinny canals, offering more places for snook to hide behind and feed from.

There is one single entrance to the major canals and it is just inside Marker 10 (thanks, Frank), and the canal runs from there to the north.

Come summer, fishing from the beach, outside of the Pass, will produce some fine snook action as well and you won't have to do it in the dead of dark. Early morning, before the wind comes up, is the best time to fish between Doctor's Pass and Gordon Pass, fishing close to the rocks. And you can find tarpon at the north bar of Gordon's Pass with the spoil area to its south also offering tarpon action. If your boat is big enough and the wind is light, try sticking an anchor in at the spoil area south of the pass for mackerel. Both Spanish and kings visit and can be chummed up. Try an Ava style jig with a six inch wire leader to avoid getting chopped off.

#42 ROOKERY BAY
Marco Island

We are going to call this Rookery Bay, but in reality, this is an "area," not a single "bay." And if you aren't familiar with these waters, never try it until you've fished it with a guide several times. And then when you do, make sure the day is clear and you have a good compass with you and know where home is. And leave the booze at home for that matter. Or else you may become a wanderer and not an angler. Rookery Bay marks the very start of the 10,000 Islands.

The north point of Holloway Island, at ICW marker #47, is a fine spot to present live baits for snook and channel bass. The best time is at outgoing tide and Rookery Channel feeds into the ICW here. That channel goes back into Rookery Bay which offers shoreline hiding areas for redfish and some snook in its mangrove tangles. Trout are here in spring and fall also.

Take Route 951 South off of Alligator Alley at exit 15 and you will find a boat ramp on the south side, not far from Marco Island itself. From here, you can head into Rookery Bay as well as the many other hiding places nearby where game fish reside. Some of these waters are called Hurricane and Little Marco Pass which exit at Cannon Island, just to the north of Marco. Anchor and chum with sardines and fish with them for redfish and snook.

A tarpon highway is found at the main outfall of the Big Marco River, at Capri and Big Marco Pass, where 32 feet of water is present. And some fine snook are in this area as well. Spawning snook were found in such large numbers around Coconut Island years ago that boats literally destroyed the schools. And as you get a bit to the south, at Cape Romany, you will be at the start of the fabled 10,000 Islands, which can be reached at Port of the Islands, east on Route 41.

In some of the prior pages, we were given excellent material for you, courtesy of Frank Sargeant, as I told you before. Frank himself is some kind of writer, and his books are available to you through www.LarsenOutdoors.com. Besides his excellent books about fishing, if you think you need it, you really might get significant help from his book entitled *Idiot's Guide To Boating,* especially if you try some of his favorite waters!

#43 PICNIC KEY FLAT
Everglades City

Charlie Wright told me about this fine location and, frankly, if you want to try to find it yourself, good luck! Check out our next location, "The Watermelon Patch" to learn how to reach Charlie, unless you really are one expert navigator. You see, Charlie told me that this site is on charts, but it sure wasn't in my copy of the Atlas, nor on my blown up map of Florida.

Picnic Key Flat is at the entrance to the Barron River (also not in my Atlas). The nearest city is Everglades City and it all is in Everglades National Park.

This flat is as much as ½ mile wide when the tide is up and it ranges from as low as a foot in depth up to five feet at full tide. The better fishing occurs on a rising tide and a wide variety of fish are found here.

Want speckled sea trout? There are loads of them in the area but

Josh Epstein (holding big fly-rod caught trout), with Dad Bill, at Picnic Key Flat.

winter is the top time of all. Try a white clouser minnow fly with green added. A size 2 or 3 hook is best and, of course, the color is gold. Pompano are in the flat as well and a white jig will produce some fine eating fish. Want flounder? The time for them is winter and spring.

The coming of spring signals an appearance of tarpon and a variety of styles is used for them. A big streamer is what the fly guys throw. But live bait will often bring the best action. A top-water plug could be thrown a dozen feet by a tarpon if it doesn't get firmly hooked, ditto a Rat-L-Trap.

Redfish are in these waters and a live pilchard will produce top action from them. And did I tell you how Charlie catches some of his Spanish mackerel? No? How about "straw fishing?"

He slides a common soda straw onto his customers' line when the Spaniards are invading. Then he ties on a long shank hook. And

Jim Edwards caught this big permit using a live crab on 10 pound test line at the Watermelon Patch.

then he crimps in a weight that keeps the straw from sliding over the hook too far. The bubbles caused by the fast retrieve of the straw drives the mackerel nuts and they attack like the dickens!

#44 WATERMELON PATCH
Chokoloskee Island ("10,000 Islands")

Captain Charlie Wright (1-239-695-1074) has a fleet of charter boats at your disposal, along with a mess of kayaks for rent so whether you want to fish alone, on a flats boat, or maybe a 25-footer, he can accommodate you with a wide variety of styles. But of all the places that he takes customers to, he said that one in particular stands out as a place that belongs in this "100 Best Waters" book, so let's get to it.

For openers, since he discovered the spot and named it, Charlie wasn't exactly ready to give any exact numbers to me. But because of the wonderful fishing his customers experience here, I thought

I would tell you a bit about this place and hope that you can get him or someone else to bring you out to the "Patch." If you stumble onto the spot yourself one day, good for you.

Charlie really didn't see a watermelon here, of course, but when he noticed that the customer of the day had an umbrella which had a watermelon painted on it, that became its name.

The Watermelon Patch is reached on a 220 degree, four-mile course west of Whitehorse Key, which is northwest of Chokoloskee. The water here is only 15 feet deep but is literally loaded with permit, especially in March but October is good as well. Permit reside here the entire year 'round but those are the two "best" months. Add in a mess of cobia, "Goliath" grouper, king and Spanish mackerel, and you know why he likes these waters.

The bottom goes from soft sand to hard and it is teeming with crabs, the fillet mignon of permit food. Soft coral and brush plus limestone mark the difference and in clear water times, you may even be able to distinguish the difference yourself from above.

Wright's customers released 400+ permit in 2002 and 2003, along with who knows how many other fish. Fly fishing is his preferred method, but he will put customers into fish any way they want to try it. Among those styles would be the use of live crabs or Spanish sardines.

His favorite fly is a pink Borski slider. Tied on a 2/0 or 3/0 Mustad bronze hook, the weight-free fly wears bucktail and mylar and tries to simulate a live shrimp or fish.

#45 SNAKE BIGHT
Flamingo

As we head further down the Gulf, continuing along Everglades National Park, we reach the Flamingo Campground and just to the east of Flamingo is a place that is called "Snake Bight." No matter what you read here, please don't try to reach it yourself. Of course if you have a "Back Country" flats boat and two spare motors with a half-dozen extra propellers and a large supply of additional engine parts, you may be able to get to the "Bight." And, oh by the way, you will probably need a few big push-poles as well. That's because the water in Florida Bay averages maybe seven feet deep, but it goes quickly to a few inches and it really is poorly marked, according to Capt. Eric Bass who really knows these waters like the back of his hand. This will be the last place we write about along the gulf. Next comes The Tortugas and then we hit the ocean spots off of the Florida Keys. Last but not least will be the many sites along the ocean.

So, as warned so often already, please don't try this yourself! A lee is nearly always available in this area, but running aground is the biggest risk of all. Eric has a bunch of fellow captains who can take you into Florida Bay and over to a wide variety of favorite spots. The problem is the getting there and back, and that should be their problem, not yours. Therefore, I suggest you call Eric at 1-305-393-1113 to book a charter. He also is the Public Relations Director for Islamorada Village, and has his own fishing radio show in the Keys.

Snake Bight is a thirty or so mile run from Islamorada, to the northwest. The Bight is formed by a semi-circle of land at the borders of Monroe and Miami-Dade Counties. This will be the only location written about on the gulf side of the Keys. And that's not because there aren't any others, it's just because so little is reachable by non-professionals. And so much for geography-let's go!

Back Country boats are an absolute must so that the boat can run into real skinny water to reach the fish.

Redfish may be the number one fish found on the flats themselves and they are here the entire year 'round. A "back-bone" (jig with feather) is Eric's favorite lure for the reds. It is a flat triangle which can be tipped with bait or plastic. The feather alone often will do the trick. Top colors are a mixture of white and chartreuse. Cast out and jump it back along the bottom and you may find that something jumps right back at it!

Snook are another fish at Snake Bight 365 days a year but spring and fall are the best times of all. A "Jumping minnow" is a good lure as well as a gold spoon. For live bait, finger mullet, pilchards and pin fish are, in order, the best.

Other spring occupants of the Bight are tarpon, but some show up in the autumn as well. Try a purple and orange fly for them but chartreuse ones will also get attacked. Ditto a big and juicy live mullet.

Mangrove snapper are in all the nearby waters and live shrimp will out-produce nearly everything. But small pilchards will also nail a limit at times.

Besides needing to know where the channels are to avoid getting his propeller impaled in the bottom, your skipper will have to know the nuances connected with the varying tides here. They follow the tide changes to reach fish as water movement slows down or speeds up. You could find as much as a whole hour difference in high water time only a mile from where you are fishing!

CHAPTER 2

The Dry Tortugas
The Crown Jewel

#46 "The Dry Tortugas"
Way offshore from everywhere, Florida

Hey, it's my book, so I can call a spot anything I want, okay? And since it is my sincere opinion that the best place I ever fished at in Florida is referred to as "The Dry Tortugas," I have chosen to feature it here as my "Crown Jewel" for the most appropriate of reasons. The "Tortugas" is incomparable to anywhere else in Florida. An old fort sits on an island out here but who cares, we are going fishing, right?

These waters are not for the faint of heart. For one thing, know in advance that you may have to sail for doggone near 100 miles from anywhere to get to the fishing grounds. You also have to know that if you are weak of stomach, back, or heart, it may not be too smart an idea to board a boat that heads to these fabled waters. ('Cause land is far away!)

Way out in open water, waves of impressive size are often cranked up out here. Yes, the professionals who run their party and charter boats to this place get very detailed weather reports in advance. And if the report is for big wind and wave stuff, they gently tell you that the boat is not going to make the trip. If you paid anything up front, they either refund your money or give you

Captain Don Brewer with two big Tortugas snappers.

credit for another trip.

But aside from a storm that kicks up out of thin air, most trips are quite tolerable and waves are not much bigger than at any other offshore location. The water in this area is as shallow as 50 feet and drops down to 125 but most of the better action is at 100 or deeper. As a rule, you will be within seven or eight miles north-east from the island. The "K" buoy is within four or five miles of the island that houses Fort Jefferson and it's only 50 feet deep. The general heading from Fort Myers Beach is 210 degrees but again, don't try it!

I only made one trip here but it was the very best fishing outing I ever had in Florida, and I sure have had some wonderful ones clear around the whole state. But this one? Wow! And the funniest thing about it is that I was told that the day was, at best "Average!"

The *Miss Barnegat Light* (1-239-463-5665) is a wide catamaran, which sails from the port of the same name in New Jersey most of the year. But for some time, she headed to Fort Myers Beach in Florida each winter to fish the inshore waters during the week, and then the Tortugas each weekend. Owner Capt. John Larson has threatened to stay north every year or so but usually gets the boat in gear and pointed south in spite of his threats.

There are at least two other big boats that fish the Tortugas from the Key West area during the winter, and one fishes it all year long. Charter boats also head down here but unless the conditions are quite calm, I would rather have more boat around me, thank you very much.

The *Miss Barnegat Light* pushes through the gulf at a cruising speed of 21 knots and therefore reaches the grounds pretty quickly. The Tortugas is so wide an area that we will not pinpoint any specific set of "numbers," but since I really don't want you to try to get here in your own boat, who needs numbers, anyhow? What you need is knowledge of what to do when you get there, and other similar details.

Bring at least two rods with you. Yes, you can use what the boat provides, and it will work. But you may want a spinning rod to fish with on top for a while, instead of just banging bottom for the countless reef dwellers that wait below.

As noted earlier, there are size and bag limits for nearly every fish you will catch in Florida and since they change, I am not going to give you any specifics here. And this far from shore, Federal laws take over anyway. But check with the captain or mate to find out how they apply when you are on a "two or three day trip." As a rule, multiple numbers may apply, allowing for a "two-day" limit to go home with you. The *Miss B. L.* usually leaves the dock by 8 or 9 p. m. on Friday night and gets back in early on Sunday morning. No, you figure out how many "day limits" that means, not me. But don't even dream of trying to "sell" your catch when you get to the dock because that is quite illegal unless you have a license and you will get fined, big time. (Why do they call it a "fine," anyway? It sure isn't anything of the kind).

A typical rig is an egg sinker of appropriate size to bounce bottom from the anchored boat. A three to six foot leader is added below your barrel swivel and then a large and stiff shanked hook, maybe a 6/0 or so. Top bait, by far, is a live pinfish or grunt. You may have to buy some before the boat sails because as a rule of thumb, the "small" fish you catch out on the grounds may be too big to use as bait. But you can buy live bait at the dock and keep them fresh if you have a very large pail (garbage can size) with aeration.

Hook the baitfish behind the dorsal fin and drop it to the bottom, and wait. Chances are good to excellent that when the skipper tells you to start fishing on a spot that you just reached, waiting mouths will be at the ready. So make sure that you get down quickly before the cream is skimmed from the top of the milk bottle. (Oh, you know what I mean, right?)

Dead bait will work quite well as will cut up hunks of dead baitfish. Frozen sardines will produce but will probably be picked off of your hook before you can blink an eye. And squid will at least stay on for a moment or two to allow for some action.

And did I tell you about the shrimp boats? The *Miss B. L.* will usually pull up alongside of several working shrimp boats each trip and gather up bushels of waste material. And this "waste" is what the shrimp boats net but cannot sell. Broken or torn up shrimp, crabs, other crustaceans, and who knows how many small fish of many an origin are taken into the boat to be used as chum and bait. I caught quite a few fish on the dead baitfish they handed over, not just on the live bait that a friendly neighbor-angler let me use.

Oh yeah, how did I do? How about 15 or so mangrove snappers, a nice mutton, four or five lane snappers, 40 or 50 yellowtails, a keeper grouper among the ones that I released, plus a 20 pound cobia and a 10 pound king mackerel, not counting an assortment of other critters. And no, I certainly did not keep that many, regardless of how many "days" I was on the boat, but it sure was spectacular, and again, according to the guy who invited me, at best, only an "average" day. I know several guys that have done even better, at times, with a pile of big mutton snappers instead of "grovers" (mangrove.)

Hey, now you know why I call this my "Crown Jewel."

Enjoy The Tortugas, and do put some back to bite another day, please.

CHAPTER 3

The Florida Keys

I visited the keys in the 80's and 90's, but did my research for the book during this century, of course. And among the differences that I noticed between the decades is that the drive is not nearly as bad as it was, due to improvements to the road network. But perhaps the largest difference is that the volume of motorcycles that traverse the keys has multiplied by an immeasurable number. However, since the overwhelming majority of bikers appeared to be close to my senior year age, I must say that in all, most were very polite and courteous.

And more important than that, I have to tell you, from research and personal experience, it's my opinion that fishing is at least as good now as it was in the 80's and 90's, and in some cases, even better than before! Credit the Florida Fish & Wildlife Conservation Commission for this due to the rules and regulations that have done a fine job of bringing back fish. But perhaps an equal amount of praise has to go to the professionals, the Captains that know their skill so well. And to my fellow "tree-huggers" goes yet another round of applause for helping improve water quality.

Let's travel up the keys, from Key West to Key Largo, fishing and talking to skippers, so that we can gather yet another fine group of locations. Note that they vary from inshore to further out, so that I can give you a variety of options. You will notice that nearly all of the waters of the keys that I write about will be on the ocean side. But if you back up you will see the wonderful place called the Snake Bight, which is on the gulf side at Flamingo. And of course, the Seven-Mile Bridge joins the two bodies, the Gulf, and the ocean. There are countless spots on the gulf side of the keys, but again, I had to restrict my overall total to 100, spots, not 200, FOR NOW.

What is particularly interesting about fishing on the ocean side of the Keys is that while an easterly blow will create some impressively high waves on the ocean side, it will also churn up the usually clear waters. And at such times, fish will feed more aggressively with less fear because they can smell your bait but not see your sinker and hook as easily.

#47 BOCA GRANDE BAR
Key West

Let's not get too confused now, okay? We also have a "Boca Grande Bar" half-way up on the western side of the state out of Punta Gorda, but this "Bar" is reached from Key West.

Skipper Walt Kirchner of the sleek 65 foot-long headboat, *Gulf Stream III* (305-296-8494) talked to me at the Key West City Marina Amberjack dock about a few of his favorite spots. His boat sails seven hour trips daily and each summer it also fishes at night from 6:30 until 1 am. The main fish sought at night are mangrove snapper.

Let's head out of Garrison Bight on a 240 heading for a dozen miles to get to the Bar. A west-southwest heading will bring you to this steep slope. The area closest to land, its western side, is very popular, called "The 10 Fathom Bar." (A fathom equals six feet, for the landlubbers out there). Just inside of the bar is 45 feet and it drops down further east to 120 feet deep. As with many similar waters from one end of the ocean to the other, some of the very best action takes place right on the slope of bottom. Fish hide and pounce on unsuspecting baitfish behind any obstruction they can find on slopes. An anchored boat will swing in wind and current and if you are lucky enough to be set up just right on a drop-off, you will undoubtedly get more action this way. You will also have to release and retrieve some line during the swing, but you do what you gotta' do to catch fish, right?

Look for red and black grouper on the Bar, with a mixture of margate thrown in for good measure. The ever-present yellowtails will appear often to add to the fun. Try a brightly colored non-weighted bucktail hook in size 1 with a small strip of ballyhoo for the 'tails. Fished from the stern, you may need a split shot or two to take you down into their strike zone.

#48 WESTERN DRY ROCK
Key West

Closer to land than the Boca Grande Bar is this natural coral reef. It is reached via a 225 to 230 degree heading, eight miles from the "Bight." The reef runs from east to west for quite a distance and is at least two city blocks wide. As a result, quite a few head-boats and charter craft can be found anchored up here.

The reef line is a spawning area for mangrove snapper every summer and Captain Kirchner visits with them during July and August at night with excellent success. But a good catch of snapper is usually produced the year 'round.

Yellowtail, the party boat staple in the Keys, is the main target. Mangrove and mutton are caught each day along with some grouper of assorted size. When a cold front hits, you can also count on the likelihood of an appearance of king mackerel on the "rock." I fished with my friend Roland Hagon on the *Gulf Stream* one day during a front and we simply clobbered kings. They were close to the top and we actually selected the fish we wanted to catch. They were chasing bits and pieces of bait only 10 feet down and we had to pull our bait away from the smaller ones in order to let the bigger fish eat. My guess is that we threw back several dozen kings that day.

By day or night, most boats will hang a chum bag or two over the side. If the current is modest, guys from one end of the boat to the other will score, and the chum that oozes out of the bags will entice fish to the top and to your waiting hook. When the tide is

Grouper and snapper on The Gulf Stream III.

cranking though, as in all other water that I have fished from coast to coast, you really want to fish in the stern for top results. Barracuda will invade these waters too, and while they may be fun to catch, after a while, and after they chop your third or fourth nice 'tail in half, you do tend to get a bit cranky.

There aren't any boat ramps nearby, but if you have sufficient skill, you may want to rent a boat from any of the facilities in Key West. Just make sure they allow you to go into the ocean. Some restrict usage to calmer waters.

#49 SEVEN MILE BRIDGE
South of Marathon

This place is incorrectly referred to as the longest fishing pier in the world. But in truth, you really cannot call it that because so much of it is closed for fishing. The northern and southern ends offer plenty of space for lots of fishermen to enjoy, but it sure isn't seven miles. But on the other hand, most of the stretch of water that rolls under the bridge is fishable, and the primary targets are game fish. Tarpon are sought after at the bridge more than any other fish, for good reason.

Before you get to Marathon, heading north, you will see a motor home park on the east side which has a small trailer parked near the road. That trailer is where you go if you want to take a very interesting ride in a train of sorts that goes over and around the north end of the bridge on down to Pigeon Key. It is here where you hear some stuff about the great and modest multi-millionaire, Henry Flagler, who established the railroad that once ran from the top of the Keys to the very bottom. Much of that railroad bridge structure remains throughout your whole Keys ride, albeit quite broken up. You will also hear about how Mr. Flager was anony-mously responsible for much of the work that actually created the Miami area, choosing to name it Miami after a local Indian tribe rather than using his own name.

But back to fishing instead of history. Anglers can charter a boat to fish at or under most of the whole range of seven miles that the bridge traverses. Properly skilled, they can also launch at a variety of boat ramps as well as rent a rig in Marathon to head to the bridge. The closest ramp to the north is on the ocean side at Hog Key. And the one that is closest to its southern end is on the Gulf side, at Little Duck Key County Park.

Elaine Bern (with Captain Hank Brown) caught this 9 pound
bonefish on the Gulf side of the bridge.

The water on the west side of the bridge is much shallower than it is to the east. Most of the boats anchor close to the overhead and let the tide bring their bait or lures further into the shade of the bridge. The big problem with getting very close, besides navigational hazards that occur, is that tarpon have no respect whatsoever for fancy rods and reels. They will inhale your offering and carry you into an abutment in a hurry. You will see that some boats are barely visible as you drive over the bridge because they are fishing very close to the span.

Reading your depth finder is very important here. The tide often cranks up hard and, joined with a stiff wind, you will really need at least a 20 foot boat with good high sides. And if your stern is low to the water, count on taking some seas overboard so try to avoid such a craft.

One of the best tarpon spots is at the southernmost end of the bridge, on the east side. This is called Money Key Channel (note the major word, CHANNEL), where the water drops down to 17 feet deep. Anchor here for a good shot at scoring. There's another place that is productive much of the time and that is a short distance after the bridge starts to the north, well before Pigeon Key itself. A 20-29 foot range of water is found on the east side and may be the best place to fish on an incoming tide.

In addition to the bridge holding lots of tarpon, night anglers catch loads and loads of mangrove snappers right under the bridge, providing their boat is well lit to draw baitfish and 'grovers up, and that fishing is done when the tide isn't really cranking too hard.

#50 HAWK'S CHANNEL
Marathon

As we head up the Keys (remember, we started in Key West), without doubt, one of our stops simply has to be at Key Colony Beach where the famous half-day boat, *Marathon Lady* (1-305-743-5580) ties up. She sails from the Vaca Cut Inlet to a variety of locations, but two of the ones that she fishes the most are about to be discussed. First, because it is closest, is Hawk's Channel, which is an enormous range of rocks that runs along much of the entire Keys. To get to some of the best chunks, the boat heads on a 110-degree course for two miles or better, depending on which piece is the first one to anchor up on. During the half-day's fishing, it is not uncommon to lift anchor four or five times to travel to yet another piece of productive bottom.

This is not deep water, for certain. It is only 25 to 40 feet, depending on where you fish. Captain Craig Spalten told me that he anchors a bit upcurrent from choice spots at times, rather than getting all his anglers lines right over the rocks. This prevents them from hanging up and breaking off too often, and also gives them access to larger fish. The small critters, mainly white grunt, are all over the biggest rock piles like fleas and to get into more snapper, he sits just upcurrent from the main sections of bottom.

White grunt, for sure, are a certainty, and are easy to catch, everywhere. You can tell them from the so-called "French" grunt because they have red lips and everyone knows that the French don't wear lipstick, right? (Hey, these are the jokes, okay?)

Yellowtail snapper are the prime target at Hawk's Channel and they are present in large numbers. Lane snapper are caught in good number here. Added in are quite a few grouper, mostly undersized ones, as well as a few that don't have size limits like Graysby and Strawberries. I caught 25 or so big-eyed toros on the boat one day and in less than two hours of fishing. Fun? You betcha!

The boat anchors up nearly every time it fishes, making it easy to feel a bite. The normal rig is a size 1/0 hook for grunt up to a 3/0 for yellowtail at bottom. Fresh mullet are provided when available, as are frozen ballyhoo and squid. The guys who do best for yellowtail fish the stern with little or no sinker on their spinning outfit and a small bucktail hook. A strip of bait will flop around in the current as the bale is left open, releasing line and giving the bait a lifelike presentation.

#51 "2038"
Marathon

Instead of fishing 2 to 2½ miles out on a heading of 110 degrees, let's try for some bigger fish now and travel on a 140 degree course for two more miles. We will shortly reach 30-40 feet of water and Captain Spalten likes several pieces here that are in 38 feet of water. En route out, you will see Buoy Marker #20 at a 120 degree heading, and then the boat will go to 140 degrees and seek readings below. Craig and I came up with the name "2038" because it is near buoy #20 and in 38 feet of water.

Sure, there are lots of grunt here, but certainly snappers are the main target. The yellowtail out here are much larger than those inshore, and mangrove snapper are the ones most sought after each summer. In fact, the *Marathon Lady* fishes at night for mangrove all summer long and usually does quite well during her 6:30 to midnight trip.

"2038" stretches for more than a half-mile in width, with its rocky reef lying from east to west. Try for your snapper here with the typical two to three ounce egg sinker if you want, but many of

The Marathon Lady *produced this 24½ inch red grouper for Robert Miller of NYC.*

the better anglers use no weight at all to reach the fish. Instead of a regular hook, many use a Hank Brown jig in ⅛ or ¼ ounce size, and the color for snapper is kind of like the same thing that a Realtor will tell you, more or less — they say it's all about Location, Location, and Location, right? We yellowtail nuts like to use a yellow jig, or maybe a jig that is yellow, or perhaps a lure that is jigged which is painted bright yellow, got it? Captain Spalten likes to splice in a length of 12-pound test fluorocarbon leader into his fishing line. No swivel, no sinker, no nothing, besides the jig.

2038 also has some mutton snapper on it but mangroves are the bigger ones that are most commonly caught. For these two though, a more conventional rig is preferred like a ballyhoo plug on a 3/0 hook with a 10 foot leader behind an egg sinker. Try to dull the color of your sinker, by the way. Snappers scare easy and its shine could frighten them away. And worst of all, a king mackerel or barracuda could see a sinker flash and chop you off, giggling all the way.

#52 DAVIS REEF
Islamorada

Head six miles east on a 110 degree heading out of Whale Harbor Marina in Islamorada to reach the Davis Reef. Captain Skip Bradeen of the six-pack *Blue Chip Too* (305-852-8477) told me that the water out here runs from 90 feet deep down to 125 or so. The reef runs from north-east to south-west for several miles, making it a fine place to troll as well as anchor up on. The deeper edge of the reef is best for sailfish, and the top month for them is December. Wahoo appear early each spring to join in the action. And from December through March, a fine run of king mackerel also makes its presence known.

Kite fishing is very popular for sails on the reef and because of its great expanse, plenty of room is present for a gang of boats that are after sails via the kite route. But trolling seems to be more popular because sitting and waiting is more boring to unskilled anglers than constant movement is. (I would rather sit and wait them out but different strokes for different folks, of course).

The best baits for sailfish throughout the entire state of Florida are goggle eyes (however at times, they are difficult to buy and/or net). However, a frisky blue runner will always make a good second choice.

The inside edge of the reef, just where it drops from 60 to 90 feet, is one place that Skip likes to anchor up at and fish for yellowtail snapper. He feels that more big "Flag-sized" 'tails are caught here than in most other areas of the Keys.

There are two boat ramps on the gulf side of Islamorada, but instead of heading offshore for the big guys, why not try your luck in the shallow waters nearby? You may find that a properly presented live shrimp will be gobbled by a freight train that some call "bonefish."

And if you want to rent a boat (or get a guide), you may score well with a rig from Robbies Rent A Boat in town. Call Annie Reckwerdt at 1-877-664-8498 for assistance. She may steer you to (here's another bonus site) Alligator Reef. It's 3.5 miles from the end of Indian Key Channel, only a half-hour from Robbies.

Anchoring up when the water is a bit cloudy will often produce snapper and grouper on bottom. Wahoo are often on station, with some sailfish, dolphin, and king mackerel. Live bait is the way to go, for sure.

#53 ISLAMORADA HUMP CHANNEL
Islamorada

Captain Bradeen travels a course of a 135-degree heading out of Whale Harbor Marina to reach this exceptionally good range of water. The distance sailed to get there is a dozen miles. And for those who simply have to know "numbers," try setting your Loran to 14098.4 at the top and 43266.5 at the bottom. But since this can be very rough water and the seas quite unpredictable, please charter a boat instead of trying it yourself.

The hump runs from north-east to south-west and the top results come from a rather skinny stretch, only 200 yards wide or so.

Back in the mid-90's, the *Blue Chip Too* was fishing suspended baits at these waters for amberjack, and the day was very productive, as you will see in the accompanying photo. The "small" fish weighed 50 pounds and the bigger beast broke the World record, reaching the nearly unbelievable weight of 128 pounds, and it was caught at this very site. The lucky angler was Joe Gazia of Danbury, Ct.

Trolling Japanese feathers is his style for blackfin tuna, and all you need is a ¼ to ½ ounce variety to fool these football sized bolts of lightning. They range from 5 to 10 pounds which means that you don't need to use monster-sized rods and reels to best them.

If you want bigger fish, troll with live ballyhoo rigged under the bill on a size 3/0 or 4/0 Mustad model #7766 hook. Sometimes the fish want smaller baits and at such times, use a short shank model 9174 "J" hook in size 2/0 with a Cigar minnow as your live bait. Rig it through the nostrils to keep it alive and productive.

Sailfish plus marlin, white as well as blue, are the bigger fish found on this stretch, and many are within the top 10 feet of water. The best depths for them are from 10 to 30 feet down.

World record 128 pound amberjack on the Blue Chip Too
by Joe Gazia at The Hump.

The water here ranges from 280 feet deep on down to 500 feet or so, and while bottom fishing will produce good results, you need a reel that retrieves line in a hurry for two reasons. Number one, of course, is that you want to gain as much line as quickly as you can in order to not get your fingers all cramped up from turning the &*@handle+?" so many times. But another reason is that if you don't get your fish in the boat quickly, you will probably only get half a fish in, because this spot holds quite a few barracuda that simply love to chop a fish just behind your hook and leave you with a bloody head.

Snapper are all over this water, yellow eye as well as vermilions. Both are very good on the dinner plate but once again, get them into the fish box as quickly you can.

#54 MIKE'S LEDGE
Key Largo

As with all of the Keys, if you head into the ocean rather than into the Gulf, and if a strong east wind is blowing, you can bank on encountering some significantly high seas. But even in a 15-25 mile per hour blow, fish are available close to land. But to get to Mike's Ledge, it would be better on your back and belly if it isn't cranking too high.

The ledge is six miles from the number two buoy out of Port Largo Canal. It is south of Pickles Reef, actually lying between Pickles and Conch Reef. Captains' Mike and Ron of the new 65-foot aluminum New Jersey-built half-day headboat, *Sailor's Choice* (1-305-451-1802) told me about the reef. The best results come in 79 feet of water and the numbers, for you who understand such things (I don't) are 2458.420N/8025.277.

The ever-present grunt can be found on the ledge in large number. Spanish mackerel are around as are occasional kings and a few cero mackerel too. Red grouper, mostly undersized, are commonly caught but a keeper will also pounce on your bait at times.

Yellowtail snapper will respond well to chum and in addition to hanging a porous chum bag over, cutting up sardines into tiny pieces and dropping them overboard will further get the 'tails up into the slick.

The stern is where you need to conduct your business for yellowtails, if you want to get them way up off bottom. A small single hook, baited with a strip of squid, or a strip of fresh ballyhoo or ribbon fish, will wiggle this way and that in the current and properly presented, yellowtails a'plenty will bite. You may need to rig with a few split shot to get away from the diving bird population and down to the 'tails, but this surely is the style of choice.

There's a boat ramp at the southern end of Key Largo, just before you get to Tavernier, but because an east wind can really beat you up, big time, please fish a head or charter boat, in the interest of safety.

#55 THE DUANE
Key Largo

Head one mile east of Mike's Ledge to reach the 327 foot long wreckage of this Coast Guard Cutter that was sunken in the 80's. Sail to it on a 160 heading from Buoy #2. It lies flat on the bottom in 130 feet of water. Her lat/lon "numbers" are 2459.380/8022.920. Heading from north to south, the Duane's sister-ship, the Bibb, sits at bottom close by, at 2459.710/8022.770. They both went down on 11/27/87, a real "Thanksgiving" for fishermen everywhere. Because the Bibb rests on her side, Mike feels that the fishing is far more productive and easier on the Duane.

Anchoring up at the wreck is most productive, but it is also easy to get permanently hung in the wreckage. It is critically important to have good bottom-reading gear so that you can find the wreck, read the way that it lies, and then determine how the current is running. (Hey, I am mechanically brain-dead so if I can do it, you can too — but the best way to fish here is with a for-real "Captain," on a for-real head or charter boat). You will need to get anchored uptide of the structure by a little so that you are in the strike zone but still not dead over the wreckage. Releasing some extra anchor line from time to time might drop you into more of the steel below, and surely will get you over grouper country. But do realize that a grouper lives there in the wreck and simply loves to bring your hook and sinker into its home for a permanent chop-off.

Very sturdy tackle is needed in this water. Once you feel that tell-tale grab and run of a grouper, it is critically important to stab skyward quickly with your rod tip and reel as fast as you can to get the fish off bottom to get it away from the many snags below.

Besides grouper, the Duane holds some of the biggest yellowtail snapper in all of the Keys. But it also holds quite a few barracuda and Captain Mike told me that at times, his customers catch more "yellowheads" than yellowtails. And of course that means that a 'cuda will chop an anglers yellowtail right behind the gill in a heartbeat.

#56 SPIEGEL GROVE
Key Largo

A 6,880 ton steel ship was brought out to this spot back in 2002 and put down in 135 feet of water. Named the USS Spiegel Grove, she stands sideways in the water, sticking way high up off bottom. Although the water is kind of deep, because of the configurations of the wreckage, dive boats may be out here so if you see a boat and it presents tell-tale red dive flags, you may want to steer away. But because the wreck is quite long, co-existence may be available. Before trying to fish it though, make sure you are in good contact with the dive boat first.

The ship was 510 feet in length, far larger than most of the vessels that have been sunk. But as I was typing this book in 2004, the 888-foot carrier *Oriskany* was about to be sunk off of Pensacola and other large vessels were slated for an underwater grave as well.

The Spiegel Grove is found at latitude 2504.000, longitude 8018.650, and again, because of the way she sits, presents lots of different angles for fishermen.

The deepest section would be where you find some of the best snapper fishing. I suspect that more muttons are here than anything else, but yellowtail will also be present. Unfortunately, where a steel wreck rests, so too do a bunch of barracuda so if you are after fish for the table, you will have to use stout gear to bring them up before the 'cuda get to them.

Stick your fish hard and once you know that you have been hooked up, reel with extreme speed. In fact, if you have one of those six to one ratio reels, bring it. No, you won't need 50-pound line but a fast retrieve will give you a chance at lifting a "whole" fish into the boat instead of a bloody hunk.

On the other hand, if you would like to take a shot at catching a barracuda for the sport of it, by all means, use a live fish for bait. Have two rods rigged, one with small hooks but yet a fast reel to get the bait on board. And then use a triple tandem hook, maybe long shank stainless steel in size 7/0, and drop the struggling offering down. A single hook will make the bait look more lively, but a single hook is, more often than not, chopped off by the fierce teeth of the 'cuda.

If you don't want to take the barracuda home, do try to carefully release it. A lip-gaffed fish will not be easy to handle but if your mate is skilled, he can help you remove the hooks and put it back. If the hooks were swallowed, you won't have to go through any of this effort 'cause the fish will have removed itself for you, with one swift "chomp!"

BISCAYNE BAY

Before we get to the "Atlantic" sites, let me pause to say that I don't have any "Waters" to send you to in Biscayne Bay. And that is not because the bay doesn't have lots of fish. It's just because this is so vast an area that to suggest you go to a particular quadrant won't be a good idea at all. Instead, take the time to find a guide up above Key Largo to take you to the Biscayne Bay Flats, which house a wide variety of inshore game fish. Permit? Yes! Bonefish and tarpon? Absolutely. But I just couldn't draw an "X" on a map for you here.

CHAPTER 4

The Mighty Atlantic

#57 BLUE FIRE
Key Biscayne

This one may be a little tricky, because instead of chugging straight out east, you will need to head south by south east to reach the wreckage of the *Blue Fire,* a 175 footer that went down in 1983. Using the Cape Florida Light as your starting point, sail 6.9 nautical miles to latitude 2534.007, longitude 8005.435 to reach the vessel. For geography lovers, you will actually be offshore of the Cutler Ridge section of South Miami.

For experienced boaters, a ramp can be found on the mainland, just below Matheson Hammock County Park. The *Blue Fire* sits in 120 feet of water and rises up 20 feet off bottom. Amberjack are the top target for sport fishermen. White grunt and yellowtail snapper provide food for the table at this wreck.

If you have never filleted an amberjack, you may be in for a rude surprise. Some people smoke them and others try to grill their fillets, but you may find out that other critters got to the fish first. And no, they aren't necessarily eating your fish, but again, some other things may have found the "A-J" before you.

You see, "worms" often get into the body of amberjacks, possibly through their mouth and maybe via their gills, but invade

Bob Sang (with grandchildren Craig and Scotty)
and their six nice yellowtails. Bob fixes reels when he isn't fishing.
(The Reel Guy 1-561-358-0287).

they do. Call them "lice" if you want, or creepy crawlers, but by any other name, the meat of your otherwise tasty looking fillet may have a few (or more) guest parasites slithering around.

I've been told that such critters do not harm the meat of the fish. And they don't damage the flesh. And they will not mess up the taste. And they may even taste good all by themselves (okay, that's a plain and simple LIE!) But to think that I will get more than I bargained for at the table, maybe a lunatic's form of "surf and turf," I guess I will just take a pass on eating some of it if that is all right with you.

If, on the other hand, you find that the meat is free of "worms," by all means, go for it. And again, I'm told that you will not be harmed at all either if you don't pick all the critters out before cooking-but you know what? I become a for-real practitioner of the fine art of "catch and release" when I catch an amberjack.

#58 " THE PIPE/BUBBLER"
North Miami Beach

The *Kelley Fleet* (1-305-945-3801) has sailed out of Haulover Inlet for many years. At times, it consisted of five boats with one or two that sailed over to the Bahamas. It now is a fine, three boat operation which offers both local half-day and all day trips, as well as night outings. So whatever you want to do and whenever it is, they can accommodate you. Being in so densely populated an area, the skippers need to produce fish and produce they do. Of course, some of the production was assisted by the addition of so many artificial reefs by the state. But this site is different than most.

The Pipe part of the name is caused because a pipe runs out from shore, north of Haulover Inlet, at the northern end of North Miami Beach, only a ¼ mile or so out from the beach. And as found up off Delray Beach, this pipe(line) carries water out to sea that has been well treated after being used to assist the town in its solid waste treatment plant. And when it is really up and running hard, the surface of the ocean literally "bubbles" as the water runs out of the pipeline. So therein lies the explanation of the two names.

The bottom that surrounds the pipe is paved with all kinds of coral and other hard material running north and south, parallel to the beach. So we have a natural reef here that is aided by the water movement caused by the pipeline force.

Situated in 90 feet of water on the first reef out from the beach, a variety of snappers are caught here throughout most of the year. But if you want your best shot at action, try a half-night trip for best results.

Yellowtail are the most commonly caught snapper on the Bubbler. But mutton and mangrove reside right in with them. Drifting is the preferred method, but night-time fishing often involves setting an anchor. Smaller boats will stick an anchor in by day but it is not a practice that is generally followed by the bigger boats, in the name of common courtesy. You see, when boats are drifting, they sure don't want to move towards an anchored boat, requiring them to get all fishing lines in and moving away to continue a drift.

Not far from this site is another location, called "Tentacle" and we will throw that in instead of counting it as another location, if that's okay with you.

Tentacle is a big pile of cut up oil rig metal that sits ½ miles from the beach off of Hallendale Beach Blvd, in 105 feet of water. I was told that some of the metal protrudes as high as 30 feet from the bottom. An assortment of bottom fish are here, such as yellowtails and triggerfish.

But frequent and unwanted visitors are barracuda. So if you are reeling a fish up and it gets very heavy, you could have been grabbed by a 'cuda. If this happens too often your choices are to fish for barracuda or just move away from the spot. Chumming at night often produces good yellowtail catches but again, if you come up with heads instead of whole fish, your captain may have to haul anchor and move away.

#59 ANDRO
North Miami Beach

A straight shot out of Haulover Cut is all you need to reach this wreck. In fact, it's only 1.9 nautical miles from the cut, to a latitude of 2553.622 and longitude of 8005.126.

The bottom drops away quickly out here and while you will be in close view of land, the wreck is going to be 103 feet down, standing as high up off bottom as 25 feet.

The Andro was a 165 foot metal ship that went down in 1985 and as with many wrecks, amberjack are the largest residents. But if you don't want them, get to the bottom and fish for mangrove snapper along with white grunt.

The closest boat ramp to the Haulover Cut is well to the north, above Hollywood, just above John U. Lloyd Beach State Park. I guess you can hook out into the ocean at the river mouth or maybe take the intracoastal south, heading under the Sunny Isles Causeway in North Miami Beach until you get to the Haulover Cut. But it sure would be easier if you know someone who has a boat docked at any of the nearby condos.

So via a charter boat, maybe one of the nearby headboats, or on your own craft, the Andro is a very short ride out into the ocean. And even though it's so close, some fine fish reside on the wreck. If it's not fished too often, or if dive boats don't clean it off, it could produce very good action for you.

Live pinfish are probably the very best bait you can use for mangrove snapper, and if you can get a baitfish through the amberjacks down to bottom, you stand a fine chance at catching a few 'Grovers. It is normally far better to fish for mangroves with long (extra long, in fact) leaders, but you really cannot do that in a wreck like this one because you will probably get pulled into the wreck. So try a two to four foot leader and a breakaway sinker. Instead of an egg sinker, use a three way swivel, with a conventional bank sinker tied onto one metal loop with six inches of leader that has a breaking strength that is half-the strength of your main line. Tie the hook leader to the second loop and, of course, your main line to number three.

If a snapper takes your sinker into the wreck, it will hang up and may very well stay right there. But with it being of less strength, it will probably break off, leaving the sinker in the wreck but still allowing you to get the fish up and into the boat. In case this works really well, do make sure to have plenty of extra sinkers — they come cheap considering a five pound mangrove may be the reward for each busted leader.

#60 DUMBFOUNDLING BAY
North Miami ("Aventura")

My friend Joe Greene (a/k/a "Tarpon Joe" for good reason) lives with his far better half, Eva, in a building at Mystic Pointe in Aventura right dead on the water. He fishes quite often right in his own backyard, in what is called Dumbfoundling Bay. This is part of the intracoastal that leads into Biscayne Bay. His building is just south of the William Lehman Causeway and his chunk of the bay is between NE 190th Street and North Bay Road. T. J. can design a business and marketing plan for you (1-305-682-1824) but would rather go fishing. He actually fishes right from the bulkhead right behind his building, the rat!

Fishing from land here is quite private, since it is in his back-yard, but you can bring a private or charter boat into the bay and anchor up and have a ball.

Joe's style involves purchasing a small supply of cheap super-market shrimp, and then attaching little bits of the peeled shrimp to Sabiki hooks with a small sinker. Cast out from shore or from your boat. It is common to catch a mess of small fish, usually pinfish, to use as live bait for the tarpon that are ever present around Thanksgiving each year.

Keep your baitfish in a live bait bucket and make ready to do some dark of day fishing. Sure, before sun-up is an excellent time, but that means that you have to get up early, and like me, Joe likes his sleep. So he fishes from dusk until midnight sometimes, seeking and often catching some impressive sized tarpon.

Rig a night float (it lights up) with a three foot wire leader and a circle hook in size 5/0 to 7/0, depending on the size baitfish you have. The smaller the pinfish, the better to use the smaller size 5/0, got it? At times, a hunk or strip of fresh cut baitfish will do even better than a live bait will. This usually coincides with cold water when the tarpon aren't anxious to chase. Use the same kind of hook but rig with an ounce egg sinker and fish bottom.

*"Tarpon Joe" on left, with guide Carl Ball
before releasing a 30 pound tarpon.*

The best tide to fish here is from full high tide on down to half-way out or so. But tarpon are always in the area at night, it's just a matter of waiting them out.

#61 BUOY ONE
Fort Lauderdale

Port Everglades is the deepest harbor south of Norfolk and if you have ever been on one of those long gray boats that have big guns sticking out all around, while anchored out in "Hampton Roads," you know that this must be very deep water indeed. In fact, it is so deep and in such close proximity to large numbers of tourists that the beautiful and huge new *Queen Mary* calls it home when in port in America.

No wonder that countless multi-million dollar yachts tie up in the "Port" as well, along with lots of charter boats and several head boats. And as you head out of the inlet on a straight shot, 90 degrees to the east, you will see the Number One buoy, 1¼ miles out in 115 feet of water.

The water crashes down to 200 and then quickly to doggone near 400 feet of water in a heartbeat as you head further to the east in this area. Captain Ron Mallet operates his rig, *Just Add Water* (954-423-8700 www.actionsportfishing.com) here often, but he cautions readers to never try it on a weekend or during the mid-day hours. You see, vessels that can eat up your boat and never even burp chug on right past the buoy. Between cruise ships and gambling boats and multi-million dollar yachts, the wake they cause can beat you up, big time. So make sure you fish here early in the morning on weekdays to help your chances.

The bigger charter boats come here to catch bait. They head right at the buoy and drift away, depending on wind and current, chumming and jigging for bait. And many of them won't really be concerned that you are nearby. It's kind of like the bluefishing I used to experience out of Sheepshead Bay in Brooklyn. Aluminum boats for the most part, would find some blues and if another boat is ten feet away as their customers are catching fish, who cares, they can move away when they hear the gentle clink of boat against boat.

From sunrise on though, kingfish, and even some sailfish and dolphin can be found within a short distance of the buoy, feeding on the abundant bait nearby. Blue runners are the predominant bait he catches, but in winter, a mess of live ballyhoo may go into your live well also. Make certain that your engine (preferably two engines) are smoothly running in case you need to move away quickly when fishing here. But for sure, count on Buoy One as a fun place to fish because of the assortment of game fish that can be taken here, so very close to land. Live bait fishing on a drift is the only way to go.

#62 THE MERCEDES/REBEL DRIFT
Fort Lauderdale

To get here, head out of Port Everglades, and travel north. Or if sailing from Hillsboro Inlet in Pompano Beach, turn to the south. But since the prevailing wind is more often from the south, bringing a boat up north, let's start this drift from Port Everglades if that's alright with you.

Ideally, you are looking for a 5-10 mile an hour wind straight out of the south. Alternatively, the same speed from the north is okay as well. From the south, head three miles north beyond Buoy One across a series of artificial reefs. There's lots of stuff down there, courtesy of the State of Florida, in cooperation with a whole bunch of forward thinking skippers and just plain nice people. A few of the better-known wrecks are the tanker "Mercedes" and the "Rebel." In fact, there are upwards of forty known ships resting on bottom in a ten mile stretch and that's lots of bottom to bring snapper and grouper.

Captain Mallet likes to run a drift in these waters, using live bait. If the wind is too modest, he will "Power Drift," meaning that by manipulating his engine, he can artificially move the boat, creating further interest to waiting mouths below.

The waters fished range from 80 to 140 feet in depth and in a westerly wind, pushing him out more, when he gets deeper, if fish aren't still biting, he will crank up and try it again from shallower water.

Besides the kingfish, and occasional sailfish and dolphin he finds here, quite a few barracuda are present. Fishing this area one day, I watched an angler who was nailed into a beast of a 'cuda struggling to best his catch. But the private boat owner didn't seem to have anyone who knew how to handle a gaff. And as the operator backed down to get closer to the fish, the "mate" took four, and then five swings, and finally on the sixth stab with the gaff, he got the 20 pounder over the gunwale. Of course our headboat was only 25-50 feet away at the time, but our skipper found the experience so funny that he wanted us all to see the difference between a pro and one who surely wasn't one.

Besides the suspended game fish we just discussed, as you cross over the wrecks, count on hooking an assortment of snappers, as well as grouper and triggerfish on deeper baits. As already discussed in several other wreck sites, try to use a breakaway sinker knot with your hook tied on a leader above the sinker. In this case, if the sinker hangs in wreckage, your hook may still be exposed to a waiting mouth and you may be able to haul a nice fish up after breaking off the weight.

#63 THE SLAB
Fort Lauderdale

Heading out of the Fort Lauderdale Inlet, one need only hang a left and travel north less than five miles to reach this spot. The Slab is also fished by boats which sail south from Pompano Beach, out of Hillsboro Inlet.

Some call this area Commercial Boulevard because a fishing pier juts out into the ocean offshore of the street bearing that name in Fort Lauderdale. While the pier may not produce spectacular results too often, the water a mile or so out from it sure does cough up a considerable number of fish. But technically, the best waters here lie between the pier to the south and a large pointed tower a bit to the north.

The primary fish gone after here is the king mackerel, especially early each morning. At times, these speedsters invade the water and tear up everything in their path. But since I prefer to fish at or close to bottom, and because kings usually are found much higher up, let me tell you about a four hour sailing I took on the *Helen S VI* from Pompano Beach (954-941-3209) during a morning sailing in February of 2004, okay?

Using my typical outfit, a bait casting rod and reel with a full load of 20 pound test white mono, I dropped a two ounce egg shaped sinker down to the bottom. The sinker was stopped by a dark barrel swivel and below the swivel was a six foot 20 pound test leader that had my ¼ ounce yellow bucktail tied on. Two tag hooks were bent in behind the bucktail hook in size 2/0. The sardine fillet that you will read about often in this book was stretched across the three hooks in a life-like presentation.

Needless to say, I got stuck in bottom several times by the three-hook deal that bounced along bottom, courtesy of the two ounce sinker and the continuous release of line that I always do as the boat moves in the current. And yes, I got broken off in the coral a few times, but did I catch fish here? You betcha!

I kept four small Graysby grouper for dinner, and also took home three of the four fine yellowtail snappers I caught to give to a neighbor. In addition, another neighbor got the three pound rainbow runner I had as well as a Cero mackerel and a brilliantly colored member of the Wrasse family that the skipper called a Spanish hogfish. I filleted a two-pound gray triggerfish at home for my business partner so my cooler was full indeed on the ride home. In addition, I released a five-pound or so undersized African pompano, plus three grunt, five squirrel fish, and a short yellow-mouth grouper. So while eight or ten king mackerel were boated, to maybe ten pounds by the other anglers, I preferred to catch ten different kinds of bottom dwellers. Oh yeah, scratch that and make it eleven! I also put a blue runner back during one drift.

The prime water off of Commercial Boulevard sits a mile or less out and its inshore edge is as shallow as 50 feet and drops down to better than 100 only a short distance offshore.

#64 LOWRANCE REEF
Pompano Beach/Fort Lauderdale

The 435 foot freighter, Mazon, went down to the bottom in 200 feet of water back in 1984 and shortly thereafter, a variety of fish showed up, and at different levels, to please folks who want a little bit of everything, all at one site. A combined effort of U. S. Navy Seals, working with local officials, fishing clubs, and countless volunteers, and the State of Florida, pulled together to help clean and then lug the tired and terrible eyesore out of Port Everglades and sink it. Local metal workers provided a great deal of assistance. The reef was named "Lowrance" as a thank-you to that fine company for the financial assistance they provided to help create this excellent artificial reef site. Volunteer tugs brought the ship out to sea while hundreds of small craft and dozens of private aircraft watched.

Parts of the ship stick as high up off bottom as 70 feet and therein lies the primary reason for so many different species of fish being here. Amberjack, one of the main fish found at most big wrecks, are commonly caught at the Lowrance. But another fish that swims well off bottom is out here, the jumping fool, dolphin/mahi-mahi. Add in triggerfish way down at bottom and you have all kinds of fish to seek.

The wreckage is located 7.9 miles northeast from the Port Everglades Inlet at Fort Lauderdale, at latitude 2613.202, longitude 8003.640. It is actually a little closer to the Hillsboro Inlet at Pompano Beach on a southeast course.

If you are on your own boat, check out the bottom first when you arrive at the numbers. It is important to run a circle or two around the wreck to see how she sits at bottom before anchoring up.

As you cover all parts of the wreck, look for suspended fish, at the high spots of the wreckage. If you can see clear and distinct marks, they are probably amberjacks. And if you also spot readings way up high, get your knees to stop knocking and make sure you have a rod rigged specifically for dolphin before setting anchor. Of course if you are on a charter boat, you won't have to go through all of those dramatics, but since the wreck isn't far out, a private boat of size isn't too bad an idea. Just be certain that you have at least 600 or more feet of anchor line with one of those heavyweight plastic floats that assist in getting your Danforth anchor out of bottom later on.

If dolphin are present, all you need is a medium weight spinning rod with monofillament as light as 15-20 pound test. Go as simple as possible to avoid scaring them off. Use the head half of a sardine as bait instead of a whole one, especially if the dolphin are schoolie size. A heavy shank hook may be your best bet because dolphin are out of the water, leaping to escape, nearly as much as they are underwater, swimming this way and that. And the more they jump, the more they may tear a light hook out so go heavy, maybe a size 4/0 short shank. Start off with a ¼ ounce rubber core sinker, three feet above your hook, until the fish come up near the top, and then remove the sinker and fish "sinker-free."

If you do hook a dolphin, try to avoid the temptation to scream "gaff" right away. Yes, it's tough to do, but if you keep a dolphin on your line, in the water, more often than not, another one or two, maybe more, will then appear, and your companions can throw bait to them. And now it's time to get your prize into the fish box.

Some people like to cast lures for the dolphin that show up once number one is hooked. A combination of chrome and feather is the best way to attract them, and a variety of such spoons are available. Just check at the nearest tackle store for suggestions.

#65 SNOWY GROUPER LAND
Pompano Beach

The *Fish City Pride* (1-954-781-1211) sails out of Hillsboro Inlet several times each day and when the wind is very, very light but steady, she sometimes heads offshore to Snowy grouper land.

A Snowy grouper is lighter in color than most other family members and is mottled with white or off-white spots throughout its body. While it's easy to confuse gray, black, Nassau, gag, and even yellowmouth from each other, you will always recognize a "snowy" after you see your first one. Another spotted grouper is the "Kitty Mitchell," but this is reddish-brown in color with loads of small spots. The "snowy" is greenish-brown with larger spots, kind of like snowflakes, I guess, thus the name.

Rules and regulations change often, but when I cranked this book out, there was no size or bag limit on Snowy's. Suffice it to say that you should never, not ever, take more than you need and if the fish is small, I suggest you try to safely release it. This is indeed difficult to do though because most Snowy's are caught at bottom in water depths ranging from 200, way down to 500 or more feet below.

If you have never tried to release a grouper, any grouper, ask the mate or captain for advice. They get the bends when pulled from water as shallow as 75 feet so they have to have their air bladders gently pierced to assist them in the recovery process.

The water drops deep pretty quickly when you leave Hillsboro Inlet, crashing down to 200 feet only two miles out and gets lots deeper in a hurry. No one in their right mind would give me exact loran numbers but I was told that rocky/coral bottom is liberally scattered both to the north and south of the inlet.

A whole sardine is the bait of choice, with an egg sinker of sufficient size to carry you down. If your outfit, rod, reel and line is heavy, you might even want to try to drift with a bank or "flat" sinker taking your size 6/0 circle hook to the bottom.

Often called a "tube snapper" in jest or anger, another fish sits down there competing with the grouper and these fish, by name, "sand tile fish" make for good eating, I've been told, if big enough. However, they are a nuisance more than anything when you want grouper. More commonly called "sand eel" a bit to the north, its different names for different folks, I guess and if you've ever eaten a true tile fish, you might also want to fillet a sand tile and check it out. But I hasten to warn you that they have an incredibly sharp point protruding out of each gill plate that can cut you in a hurry!

Remember, pick a boat that knows these water and for sure, you will need little or no wind to score at Snowy Grouper Land.

#66 THE DELRAY OUTFALL

I didn't really know what to call this very fine spot. I guess I could have said "The Delray Dump," but that isn't a very appealing name. In fact, the spot is the outfall of the Sewerage Treatment facility that covers the two adjoining towns, Delray Beach and Boynton Beach, but since it runs a mile straight out from Atlantic Avenue in Delray, it wears the name "Delray," got it?

I spoke to one of the officials of the wastewater treatment facility that operates this site, Dennis Coates. He told me that the effluent is well treated before being released into the ocean. It first gets chlorinated and then to make it safe for the ocean, is de-chlorinated. We old-timers may remember the commercials that the first George Bush ran against the Governor of Massachusetts, Mike Dukakis, which pictured the then nasty waters of Boston Harbor where such effluent was not well

*"Slim" Scranton caught this 14 pound cobia
near The Delray Outfall.*

"treated" at all before Dukakis became Governor. Well, this spot gets well treated before any release occurs.

To reach this area, you need to head south out of Boynton Inlet. Headboats from Lantana and Boynton are just about equally as close to the site. It takes about ¾ of an hour to get here by drift boat. Charter craft can make it in less time.

The water runs from 60-80 feet deep, and current generally is not too swift. On many days, you can actually see the release point on top of the water because a large swirl is clearly visible. The pipe line goes underwater a mile or so out from the beach.

Some smaller boats anchor near the outfall, but most guys simply drift. The drift is usually started south of the boil in a north wind and short distances are covered along the coral bottom below. Drifts are also set up just inshore of the spot because here too, rock lines much of the bottom and bottom dwellers are often present in good number.

King mackerel are caught on a drift here in the usual manner, just hanging a whole sardine down on a three-jointed hook with a half-ounce of lead to carry you down a bit. Release two hundred feet of line slowly and stop letting out line. Some anglers like to jig the rod a bit and others just hang on and wait for the screaming bite that often takes place. Drags must be opened in case this takes place or else a light line can be snapped or a stout rod be broken.

I prefer to fish this location while drifting at bottom. The fish of choice is yellowtail snapper, but we also get some nice mutton snappers. I've seen grouper taken here and a log-length barracuda is always possible. My standard rig is a ¼ ounce yellow bucktail, with two tag hooks added. A fillet of sardine is draped across all three hooks to present a life-like strip. Drop the whole deal to the bottom with a one to two ounce sinker, stopped by a barrel swivel, getting you down. A three to six foot leader runs behind the barrel to your three hook set-up.

Release line in the current to keep up with the drift, staying at bottom as much as you can because that's where the snapper live.

Triggerfish and porgies often bite on these offerings and for good eating, a fillet of trigger may be even better than the snappers.

Of course you may also get nailed by a high-up swimming dolphin (mahi-mahi, not "flipper,") but you catch what you gotta' catch, right?

#67 VERMILION ALLEY
Offshore of Boynton Inlet

I gave this area the name "Vermilion Alley," because I couldn't think of anything else to call it. In fact, there are many places off the east side of Florida which are called home by what is the most commonly caught snapper from Sebastian Inlet on down to the waters offshore of Fort Lauderdale.

Called "red-eye" by some, "Beeliner" by lots of people, "California red" by others, and "red-snapper" in error by those who want to sell "red snapper" to fish lovers, the common name is Vermilion snapper. And they are caught in waters that range from 60 feet to 300+ in depth and now, let's head out of the Boynton

Inlet and catch a mess of them.

Let's go over range again. I've caught upwards of 1,000, maybe more, out of the Fort Pierce, St. Lucie, Jupiter, Palm Beach, and Pompano Beach inlets, but for now, sail with me from Boynton, okay? Boats leave this inlet from two directions. They are just about as close to the inlet when they leave Lantana to the north as they are via Boynton Beach docks to the south. Charter boats as well as driftboats target them. But for sure, one need only sail two miles straight east, maybe even less than two miles, to reach Vermilion Alley.

Most of the better action occurs a few miles south of the inlet, but I've also done well a bit to the north, maybe a mile or two up the beach. If weather permits, a private boat run by an expert can be out there in a heartbeat and into fish minutes later. Again though, if you aren't an expert boater, stick to the headboat or charter rig because the inlet itself is often wild with waves crashing this way and that.

I sailed on the *Lady K* from Lantana one afternoon in 2004 and we really had a fine day. Close by was one of those small boat guys I told you about. Often seen at sea in the winter, the guy in the cockpit was none other than famous baseball manager, Felipe Alou, and he was nailing fish with the best of us.

You want water that is 200 feet deep, give or take a few fathoms. They get them in 300+ out of Jupiter, and in only 75 from the St. Lucie, but here, you want about 200.

The fish are modest in size, but give a hard bite on a light rod. Most anglers fish with 50 pound test mono on their stiff action boat rods and that works, of course. They have two hooks in size 1 or 1/0 on short leaders, both above the 6-10 ounce bank sinker needed to reach bottom. Everyone drifts and in a light wind, all you need do is release line to keep up with current motion to stay in the target zone, within 10 feet of bottom, to catch a bunch of vermilions.

Bait with a small piece of squid on each hook. Vermilions like it and it stays on the hook well. The last thing you want to do is reel up 200 or more feet of line to find both your hooks cleaned of bait so squid is tops. However, I vary this a bit. I use longer leaders to help attract the fish better, and one of my hooks is at the sinker knot, dropping a foot below the lead. And I add a small piece of cut sardine to the hook. This adds smell and shine, two excellent means of attracting a fish to your baited hook so far down in the water.

Mixed in with the vermilions often are red grouper, and at times, a snowy grouper or maybe even a Kitty Mitchell grouper. An assortment of jacks is another possibility. Last but not least are triggerfish, one of my favorite eating fish in the ocean.

Enjoy "Vermilion Alley," but make sure to obey bag and size limits, please.

#68 OFFSHORE OF LAKE WORTH PIER

Our venue after this next site is the pier itself, but before we walk out onto it, let's first get on a charter or headboat out of Lantana or Boynton Beach. The Boynton inlet can really be nasty, but the pros manage it with ease. Head north for several miles until you see the pier sticking well out in the ocean and you will be near the grounds to be fished.

A mile out is all you will need to reach productive bottom. King mackerel are generally found about two miles north of the pier in 80-100 feet of water, maybe 15-30 feet below the surface, so heavy sinkers will not be needed and in fact, will not be wanted at all.

The typical drift boat rig is generally used for kings, a half-ounce egg sinker, stopped by a barrel swivel, followed by a three or four-foot leader attached to a three hook tandem rig. At times though, a "Knocker rig" is used. Instead of placing your sinker as just discussed, put it below the barrel swivel so that it drops down to the hooks themselves. The sinker "knocks" into the eye of your top hook and that is how some wise man came up with this nick-name. In a light drift, more kings go after your sardine bait this way than via any other presentation.

There is productive bottom here as well and some fellows will drop to bottom in search of snapper. But better bottom fishing is done closer to the pier, still offshore by a mile or more, but more east of it than to the north. If the wind is out of the north, the boat will stop straight out from the pier and drift towards Boynton Inlet a mile or so. In these drifts, you can often count on being nailed by a snapper or two. However, triggerfish and porgies are more commonly caught south of the pier and each can put up a nice battle and an equally nice meal can result.

For snapper, you want a whole sardine as a rule on a triple hook presentation but if you want to take some porgies or triggers home, go with a two hook "guppy rig" if the boat isn't too crowded. This style involves the use of a heavy bank sinker with two separate size 1/0 or 2/0 hooks tied in above the lead. Baited with a strip or chunk of squid is the common deal, and prepare to slam back the instant you get hit because otherwise, you may have to reel up and get new bait. I personally prefer to use a small piece of a fillet of sardine on these hooks, but the critters below take this off with far more ease.

#69 LAKE WORTH PIER

For those who are after continuous action, I can tell you now up front, most piers aren't the place to go. But for a nice day in the fresh air, on the other hand, head to the Lake Worth Pier for a mixed bag of pleasure. For one thing, the cost is modest. Those who aren't out to go fishing can still get on the pier and gawk at the anglers. It's a photographer's dream here because fear-free pelicans walk wherever they want in their attempts at begging for free goodies. And if you dare put your bag of bait closer to them then to your own feet, it may be time to go buy some more bait at the shop 'cause you've been robbed! You can reach someone at the pier by calling 1-561-582-9002.

While prices change, at this writing, gawkers only had to pay a half-a-buck and anglers were charged two dollars, with no limit of time either. The pier is owned by the City of Lake Worth and a franchise holder runs it. In addition to the pier, two other services are available. Right as you get to the pier, a fine crowd is normally present at the bar and seating area. By day or night, smiling faces greet you and most are holding one manner of cold beverage or another aloft.

Walking around to the south side, one enters the restaurant where assorted foods and beverages can be purchased. You can sit inside or out, depending on your preference and availability of seating.

But let's talk about the fishing, okay? The number one target is snook. Live bait is the style. Make sure you obey seasonal closings and size limits, of course. Some guys buy live shrimp and they always work. But others bring two rods, one to catch small fish with and the other to handle the bigger fish they seek with the live bait.

Sheepshead are found close to the pilings and a sturdy rod is needed to keep you from being broken off in the sharp barnacles. Go with a single hook, maybe something like the blue "Virginia" bend used for blackfish up north, in size 4. Live sand fleas or small crabs are the bait that's preferred, but live shrimp will always work.

The best action occurs early in the morning or at night. The water is very clear and as a result, fish don't congregate too much in bright daylight. Try a small piece of peeled shrimp for whiting or croaker.

The real regulars have another rod at the ready, rigged with a few small jigs in case a school of Spanish mackerel appears, as they often do.

You can tell who fishes the pier often by the rolling tackle store they come out with. A modified shopping cart, this deal can carry a weighted net to lift big fish up with, a tackle box, a gang of rods and reels, and maybe the proverbial partridge in a pear tree too.

The pier is found by just heading due east on Lake Worth Road, over the bridge, and then bending around into the easternmost parking lot. Watch out that you park where you are required and do make sure to pay for your parking 'cause a man with a badge is always present.

#70 LOST TREE VILLAGE
Juno

It's snapper time nearly 365 days a year at Lost Tree, and boats from Riviera Beach and Jupiter both sail here in just about the

Here I am with a 32 pound jack crevalle on the Blue Heron 101.

same traveling time because this section is nearly equidistant from both ports.

Lost Tree Village is really a condo development with light colored roofs that are easy to see from a boat. Nearly all of the oceanfront stuff is high-rise, but a kind developer (or maybe a wise town Planning Board) built a bunch of low-rises on the beach here so, again, it's easy to pick out. There are really two different groups of buildings that are visible. One is a bit bigger than the other but again, structure to the south and north is far higher.

It's much easier to see this landmark if you are only a half-mile offshore, but on the typical clear Florida day, you can also see it from several miles out. In fact, I've been on the gambling boat, *Palm Beach Princess,* three or four miles from the beach, and could see it with ease.

The bottom here is literally paved with coral. It can grab your sinker or hook and never let go, so bottom fishermen have to be careful to not use too heavy a sinker (in particular, when the wind

*"Slim" Clark holding a 20 pound Almaco jack
also on the* Blue Heron 101.

is very light). Drop down with a four ounce or more chunk of lead
and if you are on coral bottom, prepare to get it hung and broken
off. On a light wind, an ounce is all you will need and even in a fast
drift, most regulars get away with an ounce and a half or at most,
two ounces.

Yup – me again on the Blue Heron 101
with an 8 pound mutton snapper.

The best drift you can make is one that takes you sideways up or down the beach. A mile, maybe a mile and a half out is all you need. If the wind is from the north, chances are good that your skipper will head to an area that is north of the roofs, and slow down, looking for bumpy bottom and maybe fish readings. If the wind is out of the south, the boat will probably start its drift just to the south of the buildings. Much of the better action occurs to the north though, so please note this.

Mutton snapper are the fish of choice, followed by yellowtails. If the water temperature is normal, both fish will be here and many might be quite hungry. Yes, a grouper or two may also be in a feeding mood and there are always the triggerfish and porgies to contend with. Up above, king mackerel will be on the prowl, and at times, "bonito," called "false albacore" in northern states, may be

*And – here's my grandson, Joe Morea, holding a big toro
and his dad Greg has a fine mutton snapper.*

whacking your baits but if you want snapper, you really need to bounce bottom.

The typical rig is a two ounce egg sinker, stopped by a dark barrel swivel, followed by a long leader and then a three tandem rig of size 6/0 or 7/0 stainless non-offset hooks. Bait with a whole sardine, draped across the hooks. Your mate will be glad to show you how to do this and after three or four times, you will get the hang of it and be able to do it yourself. Some fishermen cut the head off and most of us clip the sardine's tail off to reduce spinning of the bait at bottom. Fresh snapper for dinner, courtesy of Lost Tree!

#71 OFFSHORE OF JUNO PIER
Juno

The fishing pier at Juno is a landmark that is used by small boat owners who are after king mackerel. Most of the better action occurs in sections a bit to the north of the pier, from a ½ mile to a

(Top) Lisa Mattiace, alongside Captain Ryan Nagel,
with a 20 pound mutton and
(Bottom) "D.J." and an 8 pound king.

mile towards Jupiter. You never know where the bite will begin.

Most of the pros use the wind to determine the place they will stop the boat and start their drift. If it's from the south then they start closer to the pier. And if it is blowing from the north, they begin the drift a mile to the north. If the wind is out of the west they usually begin in 60 feet of water and blow out. Reverse that if from the east, start in 100-125 feet and drift inshore.

Of course if they see a few boats tonging fish, throw it all out the window because party boat fishermen will go nuts if they see rods bent on another boat and their boat is heading far away from the action!

This area is good from a mile out to upwards of two miles from the beach. The water is as shallow as 60 feet in closer and drops down to 100 feet or way more, depending on the distance they travel east. Lots of good coral bottom exists here as well, making for a good variety of possibilities. Fish up for kings or down for snapper, whatever you prefer, and chances are good to excellent that you will put some fish in the box.

You can always tell if kings are biting as you approach the grounds. Just look for small, open boats, say 20-30 feet long, with large cockpits. Many are manned by a single angler but some will be operated by one and fished by another. These commercial fishermen are after kings and are real experts at fishing and driving all at the same time!

Look for a guy in the back of the boat who is wearing a set of gloves and is holding lines in each hand. In a staccato like beat, they pull each line, first this and then the other, as they try to attract mackerel to their offerings. Many are pulling baited hooks and others are just using lures. While a king has teeth a dentist could get pleasure in just seeing, the lure is often made out of soft material, guaranteed to be destroyed after a while. A weighted bucktail, died in yellow purple, pink, and sometimes green, is the attractor. Chrome plated jigs with tube hooks are coming on strong as the lure of choice.

Watch these guys for a while and if you see them pull in line, hand over hand, or via a winch, and observe them throwing fish in over the side, prepare for your boat to be stopped to join the fun.

#72 HOBE SOUND LORAN TOWER REEF
Hobe Sound

Boats out of the St. Lucie to the north and from Jupiter to the south fish this area of hard bottom and generally speaking, produce some very fine catches. One area of the reef is found at latitude

2703.880, longitude 8002.080 and it is in water that ranges from 75 to 85 feet deep or so.

King mackerel often make their presence known each winter straight out from the tower. Many of the commercial guys prefer to pull their lines at the deeper areas of the reef but I've fished the *Safari* from Jensen Beach and the *Blue Heron* out of Jupiter a bit closer to land and caught quite a few fish in less water.

While most anglers prefer to fish this area for kings, I would rather get to the bottom and try for yellowtail and mutton snappers. The big problem though is that kings just don't have any respect for a fisherman's wishes. It is quite common to be dropping a sardine or a sardine fillet to the bottom when a mackerel decides it's time to eat. Sure, they will hit the bait most of the time, but I bet I've been chopped off at the sinker at least a dozen or more times at the Tower. As noted elsewhere in the book, therefore, please dull down your sinker as much as you can because its flash signals that an appetizer is being offered to passerby macks.

But if you do escape the mackerel, there are plenty of yellowtail snapper in the rocks and coral, which line this reef. And some very nice muttons will also go after your offering. If you have a north to south or a south to north drift, maybe 10-15 miles per hour, you really will be pulling your bait through prime mutton water out here on the very movement that is the best of all as the bait slides along bottom. At such time, make sure that you keep the reel open sufficiently so that you bounce your 1½ to 2 ounce egg sinker along the bottom and your leader trails along behind.

And did I say that the leader should be TEN feet long for muttons? No? Well, it should be, as they hit on a long leader far better than on a short one. Use the typical three hook stinger rig with a headless and tailless sardine draped across the hooks. Some guys like to then add another sardine that is only hooked at the tail end of the top hook of your threesome.

If king mackerel are what you want, and the boat isn't too crowded and you asked the mate if it's okay first, try jigging for them with an Ava style jig in 2-4 ounces. Have an assortment with you but you will probably find that one that is rigged with a green tube tail hook will work best. Use a short wire leader above the jig to reduce cutoffs.

#73 PECK LAKE LEDGE
Gomez/Hobe Sound

This fabled spot is what may be the most famous place in all of Florida to seek Spanish mackerel. I talked to Willie Howard, the well known fishing writer for the *Palm Beach Post* about this area one day and he told me that he was standing at shore the prior Sunday and figured that he saw upwards of 150 boats out on the ledge! And added to the merriment was a school of spinner sharks to compete with the boaters for mackerel.

In truth, I had heard about this spot from many people but had never fished it. I stopped in at *"Grand Slam"* (561-746-0526) in Jupiter to gather details about it one day and it literally was the very next spot I was going to put in the book. But I had called Mr. Howard earlier and he returned my call while I was out, and when I returned his call, one of the first things he asked me was "Are you going to include Peck Lake Ledge?" I wish that he could have seen my face to know that I wasn't kidding when I answered, "it was going to be the very next location I will be typing up!" He did ask me to make sure that I called it Peck not Peck's, and that's a good thing because I would probably have made the mistake.

Phew, that being said, let's get you to the "lake." It isn't a lake for sure. It's in the ocean, close to the beach, in 23-27 feet of sandy bottom water. The relative calm offered at this place seems to gather huge schools of Spaniards from all over between the fall and early winter yearly. Here's a few numbers — lat 2705.755/lon 8007.342. It's north of Blowing Rocks as well as north of the Loran Tower at Hobe Sound, our prior site.

If the spot isn't being fished by a huge fleet of boats, you can anchor up and cast with spinning gear and just about anything you throw that flashes will get attacked. Drifting will work too, and if you are so inclined, and if there is room to do it, trolling will produce, but try to avoid using gear that is too heavy for the task.

I've caught Spanish mackerel further south by throwing a bare sinker with three dark red plastic teasers hanging from droppers tied above the sinker. For those of you that have caught "Boston" mackerel up north, this is the very same teaser that we use for those fish. Their southern cousins attack such a lure with vigor.

Cast out, and crank back as fast as you can, and a mackerel will beat you to the boat and gobble your lure. A few that work well are the Fish-N-Stik in green or chartreuse. A Gulf Stream in similar color will produce and it's even better with some mylar for flash. A Got-cha jig with red head and aluminum body, painted silver, will get lots of attention.

Sure you can use bait, but in this case, lures work better and are more fun!

#74 THE KINGFISH NUMBERS
Stuart

And the numbers are 2716.59/8003.05. This is one of the most popular of all the waters of the area, fished by the heavyweights who target king mackerel. A year-round spot, friend Grant Stokes told me that topwater fish reign supreme here but that doesn't mean that snapper and grouper aren't down at bottom.

Most anglers troll "The Kingfish Numbers" and they are seeking dolphin and sailfish along with the kings. Anyone who ever fishes out of the St. Lucie Inlet knows that there are two reefs situated offshore that are aptly named. They are "The Six Mile Reef" and "The Eight Mile Reef." It's a no-brainer to know that one is six miles out and the other, eight, right?

The area we are talking about is closer to the Eight Mile, a little to the northwest of its coral bottom structure. And the water here is only 70-75 feet deep or so.

Trolling produces most of the business here and argument exists regarding speed and style. Some kingfish hotshots like to do what we call "Jerk-trolling" on one of my favorite New Jersey lakes.

"Jerk-trolling" involves the angler being a real part of the team, rather than just the guy who the mate hands the rod to with the loud words, "REEL-FAST," after a fish has hooked itself. The fresh

A huge "Kingfish numbers" kingfish!

ballyhoo that is on the hook is gently pulled forward or to the side by the angler, and then dropped back. So instead of simply dragging it through the water, your bait is made more lifelike this way, as a critter that is trying to escape and it often produces some violent strikes.

Grant likes to use a naked ballyhoo, with or without a skirt. For skirt color, he likes pink and white first, and then comes black and red or blue, or red and white.

If you hook a dolphin, chances are good to excellent that another few are close by so get any other lines in the water into jerk style to further enhance your chances at a double hook-up. A brace of mahi-mahi, jumping in different directions — wow, can it bet any better? Nosirree! And if you have live bait, make sure to troll slower, or maybe just drift in the current with them. This is where the real pro charter guys shine because they know how to "Go fly a kite" for sailfish.

#75 THE TREE BARGE — (*AND COMING ON STRONG, THE WICKSTROM REEF)
Offshore of Stuart

Thank Grant Stokes, Dockmaster for the Pirates Cove Resort and Marina (1-772-223-9216) for this site, as well as for the chunk of hot water we just talked about.

Grant and I both strongly recommend the hiring of a charter boat to reach any of the waters that are visited out of the St. Lucie Inlet. For one thing, the inlet itself is dangerous, especially in a high and following sea from the east. A good breakwater was built in the 80's that helps contain wave action coming from the northeast, but still a trip out of the inlet is not recommended for the weekend boater.

Thus prepared, let's get you out to The Tree Barge, a 141 foot tanker that went down some time ago in 182 feet of water. The numbers are 2713.419/8000.270 but, again, don't try this one yourself unless you are in a big boat that can handle heavy seas. This area is only nine miles out from the St. Lucie Inlet, a short hop for one of Pirate Cove's excellent charter boats. And as noted in the caption, very nearby is another artificial reef, just put down in 2003 with help from Carl Wickstrom of the *Florida Sportsman*. Sometimes called *The Wickstrom Reef,* she was an Army supply ship that is 186 feet long. The ship lies in 190-200 feet of water and her lat/lon numbers are 2713.492/8000.324.

Anchoring just uptide and wind from both reefs is the normal style of choice, but this is a tricky deal for sure. If you get right into the wreckage with a set of Danforth prongs, you may have to cut that expensive anchor off with the hundreds of feet of nylon line that held it fast to the bottom. Again, here is another reason to hire someone who is an expert. The pros know how to rig an anchor line with one of those huge red plastic balls that pop you out often when you head back away from the wreckage and reverse the flukes of the anchor.

Drifting over each wreck could produce results but more often than not, since you are bottom fishing, for the most part, your sinker will get stuck. Either way, drifting or on the anchor, make sure to have lots of heavy sinkers with you. In fact, in case you get hung up and your hook is riding free in the water and a beast inhales your offering, a breakaway sinker is highly recommended.

I like to use a single hook in wreckage with a fairly short leader, maybe a foot or two at most. Tie it directly into your line with a strong dropper loop knot, several feet above your sinker.

The easiest way to be certain that your sinker will break off when hung up rather than the hook is to tie the lead on with two or three plain overhand knots. The breaking strength of your sinker knot will be half or less of the line's advertised break point. So if the sinker is hung permanently, you may still be able to get a big fish to the gaff.

And what kind of fish? Both wrecks are home to true red snapper! Make sure you know current size and bag limits because they change.

Grouper are on both wrecks and for these fish, you really must have a rod with a stiff tip so that you can lift them up ten feet quickly before they hang you in structure. Last but not least on the Tree Barge and the Wickstrom Reef are amberjacks, which are most commonly found in the summer. The best thing about them is that most are caught well off bottom, making it easier to keep them from hanging you up.

*Just before wrapping up the book, I heard from Blair Wickstrom who told me that the Wickstrom Reef was already producing large schools of amberjack less than a year after the sinking. He surmised that the fish had wandered over from the Tree Barge.

#76 ERNEST LYONS BRIDGE
Stuart

While I have fished off of this bridge from time to time, I must give credit to Willie Howard of the *Palm Beach Post* for the idea for this location. This bridge crosses over the Indian River from Stuart to Hutchinson Island, and you will have to park before or after it and walk to your fishing zone. Mid-river is usually best but don't forsake the areas near the bridge ends. And to do best here, you will have to lose some sleep. Night time is not as good as the wee hours of the morning so set your alarm for 4 or 5 oyem (not a.m., because when it goes off, you will probably moan "oye" if you are like me) and get out there, ready to do battle.

Pick an incoming tide, and if you have the time to select carefully, try an early morning when the tide will be at full high at the bridge at 8 o'clock or so. The last two hours are usually the best!

This is not a place to take the kids to, unless you have them tied down with a leash, because the fishing area is really very skinny and lots of cars whiz by. I remember fishing at the little bridge on the west side of the river up north a few miles quite a few years ago. In a very modest back-cast, I hooked the biggest Cadillac I ever saw. That walkway was also very slight in width so don't take a child to this spot, especially an antsy one. And you yourself really have to be careful casting. There are only a few safe feet with a bumper that separates you from the cars.

That said, this still is a very fine fishing spot for shore anglers. If you are not a permanent resident of Florida though, please make certain to buy a fishing license because all non-permanent residents of the state have to have a valid license in their possession at all times. It doesn't matter if you have a fish in your bucket either — merely fishing is all that is needed to get nailed.

And now let's get serious. The time to fish wraps in and around winter, maybe from the start of December through much of April. And the critter sought is pompano. Not "African pompano," we are seeking its much smaller cousin, the one without all those fancy frizzles that protrude this way and that from the "African." This pompano looks a lot like a permit. (Sheepshead are often caught here too.)

In the ocean, sand fleas make up the majority of the pompano's diet. But in the river, they probably eat more shrimp than anything else. Yes, you can catch some at this bridge on a high-lo rig baited with two sand fleas. But shrimp will probably produce better. And while a live shrimp is certainly a fine bait to present, a lure may work just as well. The Indian River has lots and lots of catfish. And still more jack crevalle. And while each will hit a lure, pompano often are more anxious to attack.

The old trout tout, favored by sea trout fishermen, will work but pompano respond better to a lure that is called "Nylure," in a variety of light colors. And tipping the hook with a piece of shrimp will enhance your chances by a great deal. The jury is out on what "light" color to use but remember, don't try the darker models often used by trout anglers. Go with pink, white or yellow, and always have a variety of colors to throw. My preference is yellow, the same color that I use offshore for snappers.

Go with a size ¼ to ¾ ounce, depending on the speed of tide movement, and do just as you would normally do it if you are after snook in an inlet, or brook trout in a freshwater river. Cast just a bit uptide and let the lure hit bottom, and jig it back towards you. As the jig just starts to lift off bottom, as with snookies and brookies, that is when the pompano will bite best. And if you want to take a few keepers home, be sure to have a drop-net with you to assist in lifting your beast up over the rail.

#77 INDIAN RIVER — POWER!
Jensen Beach

For sure, when the Indian River Power Plant was built on Hutchinson Island, arguments from both sides erupted, but no matter what, little question remains regarding the effect it has had on the sea trout population of the area. The fishing has been very good from the Jensen Beach Causeway on up north, to and mainly beyond the Power Plant, for quite a few years. While it may have been easier to catch a half-dozen foot longers ten to fifteen years ago (I did it many a time), I think the average size has gone up.

Captain Squeeky Kelly (772-763-4497) operates a 23' Parker that he calls *Let's Go Fishin'* in the river (as well as offshore), and his biggest spotted sea trout in 2004 went a full 9.10 pounds. And there's bigger ones still out there.

We used to catch as many "weakfish" back in the 80's as spotted sea trout but the spotted family members seem to have taken over now. There is little difference between the two, but the "spotted" (a/k/a "speckled") fish has much more prominent markings.

Let's head under the series of bridges that cross over from Jensen Beach to Hutchinson Island and travel north to the Power Plant on your right. Also visible is a string of power lines that cross the river from AIA to the west, over to the island. Use these as landmarks if you are in your own boat.

By the way, you can rent a boat a little to the south of "The Snook Nook" (772-334-2145) in Jensen Beach, a wonderful place to buy bait and lures, as well as to find knowledgeable anglers. And as all throughout the "Sunshine State," a few free boat ramps can be found on the causeway itself to launch your private boat from.

Captain Kelly prefers the last two hours of incoming tide and the first two outgoing. He wants the clearest water he can fish, therefore when Lake Okeechobee runoff is chugging into the St. Lucie and Indian Rivers, he isn't too happy at all. He looks for 3½ feet of water, and rarely fishes any other depth in the Indian. Looking for grass bottom with open sand patches via his powerful Polaroid glasses, he stops and tells his customers to cast out.

Two basic styles of fishing are involved, depending on the skill and desires of his fares. Squeeky prefers to cast "D. O. A." artificial shrimp in nite-glo color because the body is translucent and really appears to be a live shrimp in the water as he pops it along the sand bottom. He also likes to add some shrimp flavored spray to the body for extra attraction, as well as to mask or eliminate any other smell that may be on his angler's hands.

For the newcomers, he suggests casting to a likely spot with a popping cork, fished just off bottom with a light split shot sinker and a size 1 or 1/0 Kahle (we used to call them "English") hook in gold color. Twitching the cork will add more movement to the live shrimp that he hooks on, making a wary trout forget about caution and attack.

Some of his favorite areas in the river are from 1½ to 3 miles north of the Power Plant. On the east side of the river, look for Little Mud Creek. Before "9/11," he preferred Big Mud, but that has been roped off for security purposes. Herman's Bay is another east side favorite, as are "The Sailfish Flats."

And about three miles above the Power Plant is Bear Point which is marked by a free fishing pier. You can fish from the pier as well as wade to the bird roost at the end of the point where it usually is his favorite 3½ foot depth. Cast your "Trout tout" here, first to your left, then half-way left, straight out, and start the arc to the right, to cover as much water as you can. Make sure you reach bottom and jump it back to where you stand.

So we have boat fishing, pier fishing, as well as wading. Kelly prefers to do it from his boat, and so do I. However, waders produce on the west side by parking in designated parking areas and walking out off of Midway, County Line, and Walton Roads. Boat fishing in this area is best between marker buoys 209 north down to 216 to the south.

An occasional tarpon and snook might also inhale your offering, and smaller critters like ladyfish and small mangrove snappers are always a possibility. But for spotted sea trout, check out the waters a little north of the Power Plant, okay?

#78 THE U.S.S. AMAZON
Fort Pierce

While it wasn't well known back then, German submarines sank many a ship during World War II. We have lots of them lining the bottom to the north, and one that sits on bottom off of the coast of Florida is the cargo ship called "Amazon." She was longer than 200 feet and is well broken up by now, but quite a few bottom fish call it home. And as noted at our next site, sailfish are also found up above the wreckage.

Captain Glenn Cameron of the charter boat, *Floridian* (1-772-464-

8739) will anchor up at the Amazon for customers who like to fish for snapper and grouper. In the spring, the run of mutton snapper that appears at this wreck is often quite impressive. Mangrove snappers are present along with grouper most of the year.

And cobia, sometimes big cobia, are present. You can tell that a cobia has hit you most of the time. Sure, some are at bottom, but many are simply cruising around, looking for an easy meal. And as you are reeling up, as close as ten to twenty feet below your boat, something stops you from reeling any more. That could just have been a cobia that wanted to eat your bait before you could lift it into the boat.

If you have chartered the *Floridian* for a whole day of fishing, my guess is that if you beg long and loud enough, in advance, Captain Cameron might split your charter for you. He may try trolling half the day and then anchoring up so that you can bring some good eating fish home to the grill.

The Amazon sits on the very edge of the slope of bottom that drops down to 200 feet soon, on the inshore part of "The Triangle." The ship rests on its side and offers lots of steel with crustaceans thereon to attract baitfish and the resulting bigger critters who want a free meal.

#79 THE TRIANGLE WRECKS
Fort Pierce

Not really an appropriate name any longer because there now are more than three vessels at the bottom in this area, but nevertheless, Captain Cameron told me that this location bears such a name.

To reach these waters, he takes a 120-degree heading out of the Fort Pierce Inlet. We just talked about the Amazon as a bottom fishing hole. But the Amazon forms one corner of the "triangle" around which Glenn steers his sturdy craft in search of the elusive sailfish population. When I say "elusive," this is not always the case around Fort Pierce, by all means. While Stuart calls itself "The Sailfish Capital of the World," at times, Fort Pierce produces as many or more sail catches.

In just one day alone in 2004, the *Floridian* produced 21 actual sailfish catches. Not hook-ups. Not bites. Not what we used to call, tongue in cheek, "early releases" either. These were 21 fish brought to the boat and properly released, and they were nailed while trolling naked ballyhoo on top on 20-pound conventional gear.

An entire ecosystem is available here as a result of the placement of at least four vessels (three being old tugboats) in the 1980's by the Fort Pierce Sport Fishing Club, in conjunction with the state of Florida. Adding these boats offshore of the Amazon makes for a mile of water that brings lots of baitfish this way and that, with sailfish chasing them that way and this, and fishermen aplenty joining in with the fun.

The "Triangle" is reached 12 to 13 miles offshore from Fort Pierce. Winter is the prime time for sailfish, but some are here the whole year 'round. Dolphin are the second most commonly caught fish via trolling, with some kings and wahoo as well. The water here slopes quickly from 90 to 200 feet in depth.

#80 FORT PIERCE INLET — SNOOK!
(+ FLOUNDER)

Before we head offshore, let's go after some snook with Jack Graham. (More about him in the next location). He fishes the inlet via a boat, but also has taken them from the south side jetty that is often lined with anglers casting out for snook. In fact, one day back in the 80's, I stopped there at sun-up and saw a pile of 15-25 pound fish on the jetty that had been nailed by anglers.

Jack, as with most serious snook fishermen, is a catch and release guy. He uses a bullet-head bucktail in 1½ to 2 ounce size. The color is usually chartreuse with a red tail. But at times, he catches his fish on live bait. At such times, he uses a fish-finder rig with an egg sinker and a fluorocarbon leader to camouflage his size 5/0 short shank tuna hook. For live bait, he prefers pin fish but a good second choice would be one of the countless mullet that are always present in the Indian River.

The period from February through early spring has produced best here, but no matter when you fish, please make sure to read

Night time "snooking" ala Jack Graham.

up on the laws that apply at that time, because they do change. It was these rules and regulations that helped bring back the population of snook to where it is now, so much better than it had been reduced to in the 90's.

The best fishing usually occurs on outgoing tide at the inlet, and it doesn't matter if it is really cranking hard or not. The heavy jig will still make bottom and a big mouth will often inhale it on the fly. Cast a bit uptide and as the lure bounces bottom and then just starts to lift up, more than 75% of your hits will take place.

Some fish will bite during the day but the less traffic and noise, the better, of course. Sun-up may be the top time, but Jack still prefers to fish during the night.

Catch and release your snook, or at least most of them, okay? (Note that there are lots of flounder here too and a legal-sized one could make for some fine eating.)

#81 FORT PIERCE HIGHWAY BRIDGE SNOOK

As anyone who has selected a particular fish to go after will attest to, there's something about their fish of choice that makes them hell-bent on seeking out and catching as many members of the species as they possibly can. This often means that sleep is forsaken in the interest of chasing after them.

My own personal favorite is the freshwater hybrid bass that can be found in, at last count, 28 of the states in America. And while anglers catch them best during the wee hours of the morning as well as deep into the night, I am not that nuts, instead, going after them at a slot time period just before dark that I know will be productive. But if you want critters like tarpon or snook, for sure, the best time to seek them out will be during dark times.

Relatively new to his own particular addiction is a guy I have known for many years who now concentrates most of his on-water time going after snook. And his name is Jack Graham.

Jack owned a tackle store in New Jersey for many years and then worked for the largest one-location sporting goods store (Effinger's) in the state for yet another several years. But in 2004, Jack chucked it all in and headed south to Sebastian, to fish in and around that town, but perhaps even more, in the Fort Pierce area where he has spent countless night-time hours looking for and catching and releasing snook aplenty.

Jack told me that one of his two favorite snook sites is dead under the highway bridge in Fort Pierce, in the Indian River. One of the things that I like the most about Jack is his honesty. For example, when I asked him about his hook-up to catch ratio near the bridge, he didn't hesitate to tell me it was 40-60. That means that he catches and physically releases only 40% of the snook that he sinks a hook into.

Some get off all by themselves. Still a few more will pop a line, but many more do that nasty thing that snook are well known to do, play ring-a-round a piling!

Jack fishes under the bridge on anchor from a small boat, and his style of choice involves throwing a heavy bucktail right at a bridge piling. His casts go as close to the abutment as he can get, because lots of "linesides" hang immediately behind the pilings, waiting to pounce on passerby baitfish. And while he rarely loses a lure to a cast, he certainly gets wrapped around pilings quite often by fish that know just what to do to escape.

The north side of the bridge is best, on either tide. He tries to position the boat so that most of the area he fishes is under the bridge, meaning that on outgoing, he anchors to the west side and when it is coming in, the anchor is set on the east side of the bridge, but always closest to the north, got it?

The bridge also offers a nice catwalk for shore anglers to fish from. The west side has a very large catwalk and the east side is smaller, but each produce snook for fishermen. Many of these guys go with the largest live shrimp that they can find instead of a lure. And all of them know that they need a snare net for catch and release or a weighted treble to get a fish up that they want to take home because these critters are too heavy to lift.

#82 THE SNAPPER REEF
Sebastian

Captain Hiram's Marina (772-589-4345) is the place to go for supplies, good restaurant food, and a wide variety of fishing boats to pick from. Quite a few charter boats sail from the Marina, as well as a nice 53 foot headboat called *Voyager* (772-388-0011). Skipper Brian Justice shared information with me about The Snapper Reef. A loran reading here would be 43576.8/61990.8.

The Snapper Reef is quite close to the Sebastian Inlet, easily within reach of the *Voyager* when she sails on half-day trips. It's only nine miles east of the breakwater and is rather shallow, only 50 feet deep or so. While an occasional keeper grouper comes from these waters, along with some mangrove snapper, the main fish sought are lane snappers, triggerfish, and sea bass. And since all three are easy to catch and make for fine eating, this sure sounds like a great place to fish.

Each fish has its own size limit and since it can change from time to time, I won't tell you what it was when I wrote the book. Lanes are easiest though to measure, but as for triggerfish and seabass, we get a bit tricky now. You see, for those who haven't "seen" any, each has an extra long and wiggly tail.

Most times, the fish is to be measured to its longest end. A sea bass has some overhanging stuff that is often an inch or two inches longer than the longest part of the intact tail. Some states say you cannot keep one by including its extra measurement and others don't. So make sure you know what Florida requires before putting it in the bucket. The mate will be glad to explain, so just ask if in doubt.

Triggerfish too have a pointy tail that reaches out two to four inches longer than if you measure it to the fork of the tail, as you are required to do with some critters at sea like African pompano. When in doubt, put it back is a good rule of thumb. Obey the size and bag limits and if you aren't bringing it home, catch and release is a good idea anyway.

A strong wind from the east will create big time waves, so never try to fish out here in such conditions via your own boat. In fact, get a weather report just before you try to head out of the inlet. A boat ramp is tucked in, just behind the inlet in Sebastian Inlet State Park. You may even want to try your luck from the jetty, especially at sundown and sunup. On slack water, a doormat sized fluke (flounder) might get hungry.

#83 BETHEL SHOALS
Sebastian

The Bethel Shoals Loran reading is 43440.8/61972.5 and nearly all of the hot waters are offshore of it.

Bethel Shoals may be the most famous of all the offshore fishing grounds around the entire perimeter of the main coastline of Florida. I know that I have caught more grouper and mangrove snapper here than anywhere else, and I can attest to the fact that I have caught plenty elsewhere so you know that Bethel Shoals was a place I loved to fish.

In order to reach the shoals from Sebastian, the boat has to travel about 16 miles southeast from the inlet. You can get there too from Fort Pierce, by sailing maybe 18 miles to the northeast from that inlet. Captain Justice told me that the water is just about 12-14 miles due east of Vero Beach.

It was on these waters that I first witnessed the extremely fine art of underhand casting big egg sinkers that have 20-40 foot leaders trailing behind. Such skill involves whipping baitfish out so far that you cannot even dream of accomplishing such a cast. But properly done, it can be a very impressive sight indeed. Mangrove snappers, and to a slightly lesser degree, muttons, avoid sinkers as much as possible, thus the extra long leader.

Back in the 70's and 80's, our main target was grouper, followed by mangrove snappers. But with the positive results of rules eliminating the possibility of overfishing, another member of the snapper family has reappeared. True red snapper are often caught on Bethel Shoals and I'm talking about "keeper" sized ones at that.

Captain Justice told me that in 2004 he saw more big sea bass out here than in any year he ever fished these waters. Some fish that went from 3-4 pounds were brought up and while such fish are fairly common in New Jersey and New York waters, a 1-2 pounder used to be considered big in Florida. And if you have never eaten a sea bass, do try it. The top of the sea bass run is from fall to early winter, but some are always around.

He fishes ridge lines on the shoal, looking for readings of bait before getting his anchor impaled in the 80-100 feet depths below.

Those who just want to take some fish home for a meal catch porgies and triggerfish and this style involves the use of somewhat smaller hooks baited with squid. One never knows though when a big beast will eat such small bait so get ready for anything.

Rick Smith Sr. of White Lake, Michigan got a "ringer"
at the Horseshoe with this nice sailfish.

#84 THE HORSESHOE
Sebastian

Well, we just discussed the fabled Bethel Shoals area. Now let's crank up the engine on the charter boat, *Big Easy* (772-664-4068) and head offshore further by about four miles. Captain Terry Wildey runs his boat out of Captain Hiram's Marina and he told me that he often makes a stop right at the buoy itself to catch a mess of live pilchards for bait.

A Sabiki rig is all that he needs to load the live well. But at times, he will also nail a cobia from around the base of the buoy because they love to feed on the bait pods around it. The numbers are 43440.2/61958.0 according to Brian Justice of the *Voyager*.

While the buoy is at a 115 degree heading, Terry said he really runs at 112 degrees from the inlet to get to The Horseshoe. It's a large patch of high bottom that goes from 95-100 feet for the most part, but also is as much as ten feet shallower in sections on ledges and here is where some of the best action takes place.

The *Big Easy* anchors up and catches mangrove and mutton snapper here along with lane and vermilions, but Terry prefers to slow-troll or drift in this area for kingfish in January and February, with some nice sailfish mixed in each winter on the Horseshoe's outer edges.

Use an offset 6/0 to 8/0 hook with live bait and a three foot length of leader when on anchor.

One set of Loran numbers at this location would be 43440.6/61956.

This site is a bit too far to the east for private boats that launch from the State Park. So I really suggest that you don't try to find it that way, please.

#85 SEBASTIAN FLATS
Indian River, Sebastian

The flats boat, *Little Easy* is the small member of the *Easy* fleet. In the prior location, we talked more about the bigger boat, the *Big Easy*, owned by Terry Wildey. He may be one of the only skippers who offer two distinct options, an offshore boat as well as a river one.

Terry shared details with me about two inshore locations, but we will simply call them "The Flats," and break them down a bit further now.

First comes the section known as Long Point Flat. It lies off of Long Point Park on the east side of the river, maybe one to two miles north of Sebastian Inlet. This is a huge stretch of grass with open sand areas and is only 1 foot to 1½ feet deep.

In the winter, when this water warms up by 10 or 11 in the morning, sea trout, the speckled variety, come to play and eat here, and he has caught lots of them. The top lure is a surface popper, maybe because of the excitement caused when a fish slams it on top. A Yo Zuri "Three D" minnow is one of his favorites too. This suspended stick bait is made to look like a mullet — its only color is "scaling."

He also uses a Cotee jig, ⅛ to ¼ ounce in weight, with a split tail. Jerked up and down back to the boat, it looks like an escaping shrimp and trout usually get to the lure before the angler can haul it into the boat. At times though, they darn near come in at the same time. Pompano, redfish, and snook are on the flats as well.

The second of the Sebastian Flats is found another five miles to the north, also on the east side of the Indian River, and wears the name "Honest John's Flat." It is called that because the owner of the boat ramp that was closest by had the name John and he hung a coffee can at the ramp for fishermen to put a half-dollar into to pay for launching. Honest as he was, he expected honesty in kind from his customers and they usually were just that.

Specked and regular weakfish sea trout crossbreeds are commonly caught in this area, along with the more prevalent speckled variety.

#86 PORT AUTHORITY SITE #2
(and Cargo Pier #4)
Cape Canaveral

To reach this artificial reef, your boat will leave Port Canaveral and will travel north by northeast to latitude 2830.382, longitude 8013.323 before setting anchor in 125 feet of water. 400 tons of concrete culverts were dropped overboard from the barges that carried the material to this site in 1997, 19.2 miles out from Port Canaveral. Some of the stuff rises off bottom by as much as 15 feet.

And in case your skipper finds another boat or two already over the reef, he can just chug out 3/10 of a mile further to lat 2830.129, lon 8013.142, where the same basic variety of fish reside. So even though we are talking collectively about two reefs, let's just call this one with the other, called "Cargo Pier #4 materials," as our back-up. This second reef went down in 2000, by the way. It is a 121 foot deep reef, with a profile of 20 feet, and consists of concrete rubble. Standing so tall, it must have been quite a great deal of rubble at that.

We are after gag grouper, gray snapper (mangrove) and trigger-fish at both sites. So you have a choice of going big, middle or small, depending on what kind of fish you want for dinner that night. And if the fish are really biting, you may want to have two rods rigged, maybe three, and switch over from time to time.

"Gag" grouper are also incorrectly referred to as "black" grouper. But a true "black" has different markings, and is usually darker in color, with darker fins. Make sure you (or your skipper) know one from the other because they may have different size limits. Another alias for the gag is "gray" grouper.

The ever-present grunt will be here, and it might be a good idea to catch a few and set them up for bait. The style I am about to suggest requires a few things. Maybe number one would be an uncrowded boat and a highly skilled and anxious to please mate. #2 puts the deal in your lap. And to do it, you need a boat that isn't bouncing and a super sharp and thin fillet knife.

Give the grunt a hard whack to settle it down and then partially fillet one side and then the other, from tail to an inch before the gill plate. Yes, filleting is usually done from head to tail, but we aren't getting dinner ready for you, but rather for the grouper and snappers under the boat.

Follow the bones on one side and then the other. Before, be certain you stop BEFORE the gills, then cut away the tail, bones and all the fins. You will now have a head with two flopping slabs of flesh hanging from the head. To add to the attraction to fish below you, now cut each hanging section of meat from tail part towards the head, with at least a whole inch of uncut solid meat behind the gill, on both sides of your bait.

Some folks call this a "broken-back" bait and if you look at it, and if it was set up correctly, it will bring just that in mind, a fish with a badly broken back. The grunt will have four separate pieces of meat that hang from the head/gill and each will flutter around at bottom, attracting a variety of bottom dwellers. Some of the more adventurous triggers will try to peck away at the fluttering pieces; but if you have fresh bait and did it right, most triggers will give up and look for easier food to find.

And now you have a large and tasty bait at bottom, and at any time, a gag or "mango" may decide that is time to eat. And if you did it right, a fine fish will soon appear alongside of the boat!

You should have one extra bait ready at all times because you could lose one to the wreckage and since it takes so long to set the bait up correctly, two prepared baits will give you an easier time of it.

#87 PELICAN FLATS
Cape Canaveral

Hey, there's plenty more to see in Cape Canaveral besides the spacecraft program, you know. You may also find time to sail on the gambling boat that heads out past the three mile limit if that is your thing, but for me, Cape Canaveral means the same thing as most of Florida stands for: fishing, and plenty of it at that!

And for assistance in locating a hot spot I called the *Orlando Princess* (321-784-6300) and talked to Captain Charles who shared information with me about the Pelican Flats.

The "Flats" are located between 18 and 19 miles offshore and for most headboats, that means a long ride but since this 2002 aluminum catamaran cranks up to 20 knots or so, you can get there in less than an hour!

The water fished is reached on a 115-117 degree heading, nearly due east, and one hot chunk of it is on a loran reading of 43787.5/61926.5. The water runs between 85 and 90 feet in depth and holds a wide variety of bottom dwellers.

The typical outfit that the boat provides uses a 6 to 8 ounce egg sinker, depending on current, with a 2½ to 3 foot heavy leader that a size 5/0 hook is tied onto. The usual bait is a hunk of squid or a piece of frozen sardine. There are lots of little bait stealers down at bottom, waiting for your offering, so if you can buy some fresh bait, do so, it will stay on the hook longer.

While I don't like mullet as much as sardines, a piece of fresh mullet will improve your odds, simply by remaining on the hook longer. And if you can afford to do so, a package of fresh ballyhoo will really produce excellent results. Try filleting the bait fish and putting strips on the hook. Another option would be to just put fresh chunks on.

The *Orlando Princess* anchors up and as soon as the word is put out to drop down, you had better be ready, because the moment you hit bottom, you should be in business in a hurry. And at times, the biggest fish will be the first ones to eat.

True red snapper are here, along with muttons and mangroves. Some yellowtail snappers can also be caught but there are far more lanes and at times vermilion snappers than yellowtails. Gag and black grouper are on the Flats and some are legal size. And if you like sea bass, expect to take a few tasty keepers from these waters.

Triggerfish as well as grunt will try to pick your hooks clean but if you catch a good-sized trigger, make sure to bring it home and try it out. If you haven't cleaned one yet though, ask the mate to do so for you and don't forget to tip him. You have to stick a sharp knife point in to get the fillet started and then it's quite easy. But if you don't know how to begin the fillet, you will cuss me out, big time.

A good run of king mackerel appears each summer, and at such times, it is preferred to make certain that your sinker is dull in color, or prepare to re-rig from time to time. As the sinker is dropping to bottom, kings will attack the flash and belt it, cutting your line in a heartbeat. Seriously, as noted several times already, try to rub your sinkers in dirt or mud or somehow or another, find a way to remove the shine.

#88 "MANGRO" HOLE
Ponce Inlet

Captain Carver of the *Critter* Fleet told me that "Mangro," one of the many nicknames for mangrove snapper, was given to this place quite a few years ago. In some areas they are referred to as "Mango," and elsewhere, as "Grovers," but by any other name, a mangrove snapper is a fine fighting and good eating member of the clan. Just be careful and avoid their nasty overbite, because those teeth can chomp a finger, hard!

The all day member of the *Critter* Fleet sails 29 miles out on a 65 degree heading to get here and a mid-reef loran reading would be 44384/61812.5. The inshore end of the reef is 97 feet deep and its offshore side is 105 feet below.

Some boats troll in this area for wahoo and barracuda but anchoring will produce some very nice catches. Some outsized gray grouper reside on this natural reef and African pompano to as big as a full 30 pounds will take your bait at times. But the reef is named "Mangro" for a good reason. That is because most guys are after mangrove snapper here and they are often caught in good number.

Mangroves, like their clan-members, muttons, are sinker shy. Use the lightest egg sinker that can take you to the bottom and add a long, long leader. 10 to 12 feet is the minimum you should use in 60-80 pound test to reduce the number of cut-offs in the rocks. The typical mangrove is 2 to 3 pounds but 4-6 pounders are quite common. However, a 15-20 pounder will often win the pool and is always a possibility.

Big vermilion snapper are on the reef, with ever-present grunt, porgies, triggerfish, etc. Hey, Lee said that he calls the place "The Zoo" because it holds just about every kind of fish on it.

Rainbow runners will swim at mid-level, chasing after the vast numbers of bait fish that you can catch yourself on a Sabiki rig. But keeping them alive is another thing unless you have an aeration system set up alongside of you.

Cobia are taken at a variety of levels and barracuda, some log-length beasts, often roam around and practice their fine art of snapper chopping. It is quite common to be reeling up a fine snapper to only find that half a snapper is all you lift into the boat.

In recent years, some guys have taken and adapted the Keys method of fishing for snapper, by eliminating the sinker completely and fishing a jig or plain old bait fish. Most of this is done in the stern and chumming with bits of sardines will bring mangrove and mutton snapper up high enough to be caught on lighter gear.

Try a red jig head with a 1/0 hook and a strip of fillet out of a fresh caught fish. A sardine hooked in the snout will work well but you may have to pick through the rainbow runners that will be on station.

Lee's personal favorite style involves fishing for mangroves with a "plug." Talked about before at location 23 (The Sheridan), this is usually a just caught grunt that he cuts the head and tail off of. Then he scissors the fins off around the whole fish. What remains is a "plug" — a chunk of fresh meat that is just about impossible for a small fish to either remove from your hook or eat a piece out of.

It stays at bottom and the "grovers" will usually respond with one of their patented long and speedy runs. When your long leader signals that you are in business, it is then time to separate the fish from the bottom with a long and hard sweeping strike to the sky.

#89 PARTY GROUNDS
Ponce Inlet

These waters are called "Party Grounds" because this is a very popular place for party boats. The Gulf Stream is very close to shore from Jupiter on south, but from Jensen Beach north, you really have to ride a good distance to reach blue water. However, the boats that head out from the more northerly parts of the east coast of Florida have lots and lots of excellent structure to fish on top of, blue water or not, and that's the bottom line to anglers who like grouper and snapper fishing.

The *Super Critter* (386-767-7676) fishes here on its half-day trips and will often see a few dive boats on the reef. This is a "natural reef," and the bottom has a good deal of material that fish like to pick a meal out of.

Coquina is one of the natural structure and sea fans aplenty are down there. Sea fans are very popular hiding places for small crabs and shrimp. A patient fish will set up shop and bang headfirst into them and try to knock a meal out. Triggerfish in particular like to do this and the reef has queen as well as common gray triggers. (A "Queen" has wonderfully colorful markings, blue with green, while a "common" is just that, plain, dull gray.)

The Party Grounds are fished from anchor, as are all of the spots in this section of the state. It is 17 miles from the inlet and is reached on an 80 degree heading, three miles beyond the "Cracker," our next "waters."

Look for gray and gag grouper, with plenty of snapper on this spot. White-boned porgies join with sea bass and northern anglers in particular know that both fish make for good eating. The water depth here is 80 feet and is not far down when you release your baited hook, but is certainly a long distance up if you have a fine grouper tugging. Therefore, if grouper or big snapper are what you seek, please have a rod with a sturdy tip so that you can haul them

A typical day on The Critter – *triggers and snappers.*

up quickly before you get snagged. The boat will provide the kind of rod and reel needed if you don't have your own gear. Please don't even dream of bringing a long and skinny surf stick with you though, as you will create all kinds of grief among your fellow anglers with one if you do happen to hook a big fish.

At times, a goodly number of true red snapper are found on the Party Grounds. Most will be under the size limit but enough will make it to keep things interesting.

#90 CRACKER REEF
Ponce Inlet

Daytona Beach is a much more famous name, but for folks who like to hit the ocean in Florida, Ponce Inlet is better known by far. And one of the reasons for that is that the famous *Critter Fleet* (386-767-7676) sails out of this inlet. Discussed in our two previous locations, the fleet is located at 4950 So. Peninsula and the docks are a short hop to the open water. A half-day head boat plus an all-day one are here, along with five charter boats so you really have lots to select from for a day of fun.

A 14-mile sail brings you to this relatively close-in artificial reef and in the summer, it is visited by lots of reef dwellers. Sea bass invade its bottom structure when it gets cold and at times, they are so numerous that it's tough to get a bait to anything else. And if you have eaten the perfectly white and tasty fillets out of a 3 pound blue nosed sea bass, you know that you may not be concerned about that at all.

Captain Lee Carver operates one of the *Super Critter* boats, and told me that he sails on an 80 degree course (east by north/east) to hit the 70 foot waters of the Cracker Reef. A mid-area of it is on Loran reading 44409.1/61959.0.

A vast area of bottom is paved with every kind of material imaginable. A drawbridge was taken down and replaced and the old material was cleaned and then barged out to this spot to be dumped overboard, creating a wonderland of structure below. Six foot road culvert pipes, those huge ones that you see on Route 95 that seem to always be in process of being removed and replaced pave the bottom too. Even an over the road car carrier that had carried one load too many, I guess, was donated and plopped in. A full three miles of bottom in this area has an assortment of stuff and while open sand exists, the professionals who operate the gear in the pilot house sure know how to find the hard material below. And of course they all have their own "book of numbers" to rely on.

Mangrove and lane snapper are on the reef, with triggerfish as well. Vermilion snapper are also in these waters. Grouper hide in and around the great structure on the reef and you may hit a real biggie here, even though it is relatively close to the beach.

#91 "BRIDGE RUBBLE — FIVE IN ONE"
South Daytona

We will shortly talk about several sites that are situated further out to sea, but let's discuss a mass of material that went down even closer in to the beach. If you remember the old term "Green Grass

Syndrome," which theoretically means that the grass is greener on the other side of the fence, well, there is plenty of "grass" closer in, courtesy of the State of Florida and cooperating transit authorities.

Situated a short hop from Ponce Inlet and waiting for you are gag grouper, amberjacks, and sea bass. Let's talk about these five separate reefs, and how to get there, but to be boringly repetitive, I would rather you go here with a licensed skipper, if only in the interest of safety.

Five separate loads of old bridge structure were put down only 6.5 miles from the inlet over a considerable period of time, and together, they make a massive volume of concrete and steel that awaits you. Since the site is so well known and close to shore, you will undoubtedly find dive boats here but because there is so vast an area covered, there still should be plenty of room for everyone.

If you would like to use your own trailered boat, a ramp can be found very close to Ponce Inlet, near the southern tip of the island. Take Route A1A over at South Daytona/Port Orange, and head south and it should be pretty easy to locate the ramp just inside of Ponce Inlet. There is another ramp off of Route 44 at New Smyrna Beach, south of the inlet.

The piles of material are a bit to the north of the inlet. Section #1, a load of concrete and steel from the old Port Orange Bridge, went down at the tail end of 1990 at latitude 2907.180, longitude 8048.320. Then at the start of 1997, 450 tons of concrete material from the NSB Bridge was dumped at 2907.189/8048.324. Two more masses of NSB Bridge material were sunken in June of 1997. They were 500 tons of concrete bridge slabs at 2907.198/8048.233 and a week later, another 500 tons were dropped over at lat/lon 2907.250/8048.253. The last of five masses of material that went down came from the NSB Bridge in the spring of 2002 when 500 tons of concrete poles were added at 2907.270/8048.360.

This entire load of concrete and steel now make up a huge volume of artificial reef in 65 feet of water, with some of it standing as tall as 15 feet off bottom.

Grouper like large baits so if you want a shot at them alone, use larger hooks and bigger baits. If any of the resident amberjacks are at or near bottom they could mess up your plan, but let's assume for now that they sit suspended. So to catch a nice grouper, use a whole sardine. Hook it through the head on a size 6/0 hook and drop it down. Sure, if you can get any live sardines or, for that matter, any other silvery critters, they make much better baits but dead bait will work well on grouper. Make sure that you slam back quickly as soon as you feel that wild surging bite and if you timed it right, it will be fresh grouper for dinner.

If the grouper aren't biting, or if you want to give your child a shot at some fish that are not too big a challenge, then just go with smaller hooks and bait for sea bass. Remember, a 7 or 8 year old isn't after size, they just want to catch a fish, any fish, and sea bass are among the most cooperative in the ocean. If you have fresh bait, cut off a hunk and stick it once with a size 3/0 hook and tell Jr. to get ready!

#92 BIG GEORGES REEFS
Palm Coast (Flagler Co.)

Not nearly as accessible as many of other the artificial reefs, your skipper may save this one for a day that finds the ocean covered with boats. Since it is a long ride to reach it, Big Georges' two piles may be available and loaded with fish.

While these two placements of material may be situated closer to the inlet at Fort Matanzas, the state suggests heading out from Ponce Inlet. And if Ponce is the jumping off spot, the boat will have a 28.1 or 28.2 nautical mile ride before reaching the selected waters, thus the idea that this may be an ace-in-the-hole due to distance.

Gag grouper, mangrove (gray) snapper, and triggerfish are present at Big Georges Reef.

The reefs are on a straight shot, more or less, offshore of Palm Coast, up near the top of Flager County. Two masses of material were put into place on 5/9/95 and they went in at 2935.880/8053.600 when 500 tons of concrete culverts and a mess of catch basins were dropped over. Another load of concrete

A bargeload of stuff going down at Big Georges.

culverts were sunk at latitude 2935.896, longitude 8053.927.

This area of bottom is only 64 feet deep and the concrete rises as high as a dozen feet from the bottom. Having so high a profile offers grouper, snapper, and triggers plenty of room to pick off crabs and shrimp, which try to hide in the rubble. And if you drop tasty bait to them, they may find an easier way to get a meal, even if it may be their last one.

If triggerfish are the "only" things you catch, don't consider this a wasted trip. Sure, you may have wanted fresh snapper or grouper for dinner, but I honestly feel that other than a small strawberry or graysby grouper, I would rather eat a fillet of triggerfish than any other fish in Florida!

Let's assume that you really know what you are doing, and want to clean the fish yourself. You will need a very sharp knife for starters, and a solid carving board. I have several of those old skinny pointy serrated steel knives, which I use to start my opening in the back of the fish. A sturdy and sharp pointed fillet knife works even better but I make do with this style and it does the job just fine for me.

Make a sawing cut on one side of the fish, from behind the eye down to below its side fin, cutting into the flesh. Then take a regular fillet knife and follow the back bone towards the tail and work your way down to the belly and remove what will be a nice fillet. Do the same thing on the other side and you will have two very much bone-free pieces of meat that you may want to trim further.

The top of the fillet may have some reddish ribbed membranes attached. These are the remainders of the dorsal "trigger"-fin. If you want to really produce the purest white of fillets, you can remove this red material with a sharp knife with ease. Just cut it away — it will not be tough to do.

A two pound triggerfish is mostly waste, but you will get two fillets that weigh about six ounces each. And after you try your first meal, cooked any which way at all, you may find that you will not want to share them with anyone else in the house. That's kind of like how I get when I start eating fresh crabs and everyone else tries to grab the little pieces of meat that I manage to pry out without cutting myself.

#93 MATANZAS RIVER
Crescent Beach

Bryan Turnquist of the Devil's Elbow Fishing Resort (904-471-0398) reminded me that the Matanzas is part of an entire network of inland waterways. So while we call this spot the "Matanzas River," we will just select a few sections of it that are near the resort that he works in at Crescent Beach. And if you want a guide to keep you from getting lost, he suggests Captain Jimmy Blount who runs a flats boat called *Scratch-Off* (904-797-9001). There are many other skippers in the area as well, of course.

Come autumn, some of the biggest redfish around appear on the flats nearby on high tide. The water is very skinny, in fact, is high and dry on low tide, and this is where some of the best action takes place on flood tide. A flats boat is needed to creep up on tailing fish in the grass and they often will respond to a chartreuse soft plastic lure as well as a red and white Mirro-lure stick bait.

Devil's Elbow is straight east across from channel marker #70, and this is a fine deeper water area to fish during most of the year.

The channel has anywhere from 10-20 feet depth and redfish reside here. Add black drum, speckled & yellowmouth sea trout, and a nice bi-catch of tasty flounder and you have a fine assortment to select from.

Oyster beds line the river and at low tide, you can see the exposed shells. If the water is not covered with boats and is calm, stick your anchor into bottom and walk out onto the hard bottom. Turning over oyster shells will produce a nice supply of little "oyster" crabs which are the top of the line bait in this area. Sand fleas and fiddler crabs that are store-bought will work, but what you find where you fish will always beat store-bought.

All the critters referred to above will inhale such a crab while you are anchored on the edge of the channel, but you also have access to some of the biggest sheepshead in the area and they sure do make for fine eating as well as a great fight.

The nearby feeder creeks produce good redfish in early spring but the main channels are best in the summer. Redfish are the most popular fish in the area, by far.

Another method used involves a ¼ ounce lead head jig, bounced on bottom in the channel, with a live shrimp or finger mullet as an added attraction.

#94 TAYLOR REEF
St. Augustine

Based purely on the overwhelming volume of material that lines the bottom on this reef, there aren't more than one or two sites in Florida that consist of so much stuff. And if bigger is better, then for sure, we have to include the Taylor Reef as one of our "100 Best." You see, in addition to 2,500 tons of concrete, fiberglass culverts and other pre-cast concrete make up this low profile mass of snarls and tangles of stone.

White grunt are there for the little ones, but your kid may find that a beast grabbed hold of his fish as he was just starting to reel up. That beast could be either a fine grouper or a mangrove snapper, because the state said that there are plenty of each on this reef.

Keep the bigger grunt for dinner, or if you have hungry neighbors, give them a few to try. White grunt are better tasting than those that have a black membrane which lines their inner stomach wall. I suppose that this tastes okay, but I don't like its look and rub it away in the fillet process with a cloth.

Cut a plug from a small grunt and use it as bait. Gray (mangrove) snapper and grouper each will chow down on a plug and nothing else will be able to remove it from your hook. Talked about before, briefly, a plug consists of a fresh caught small fish, with head, tail and fins removed. The remainder will be a long, thin chunk of meat and bone that stays on your hook forever, at least until it is eaten by a fish you seek.

The Taylor Reef is in 100 feet of water and was created in June of 1994. Being in place for 10+ years has established it as a place that attracts crustaceans, mussels, and the whole food chain that follows.

The latitude shown for Taylor is at 2955.691 with a longitude of 8050.731. It is pretty much a straight shot east out of the inlet, 23.3 nautical miles from St. Augustine. Two ramps are nearby for guys with big boats and bigger boat operating skill. One is near May Street and San Marco Avenue in Vilano Beach. The other is back up Salt Run near the Lighthouse Park Pier.

#95 21 FATHOM BOTTOM
St. Augustine

Not much of a secret spot, the real secret is how to fish these very popular waters, and I turned to Captain Glenn Laudenslager, who runs his 36' *Orca* (904-825-1971) out of Camachee Cove Marina in the Matanzas River for assistance in learning about it.

The 21 Fathom Bottom is reached by sailing due east out of the inlet, and traveling 35 miles offshore. It stretches all the way down from Jacksonville to Daytona, covering miles and miles of water. The bottom formation is natural limestone with ledges galore to give bottom feeders all kinds of holes to hide in.

But come summer, Glenn prefers to fish up off bottom, trolling, along the edges as well as right through the 126 feet of water that lies below. He pulls upwards of five lines at a time on a special planer rod he uses. And most of the time, the business end of each rod has a ballyhoo attached, with a blue and white skirt. He varies his depth and when fish are located, he will try to hold most of the baits at the same level.

Trolling will produce dolphin, wahoo, king mackerel and amberjacks, a fine variety of game fish.

Much of the rest of the year will involve anchoring up over the limestone, unless his customers want to troll. On anchor, the primary target fish are true red snapper, which have made a fine recovery in his area. A 5-6 foot leader below a heavy egg sinker, with a 6/0 hook is the style used for snapper. Grouper, gag mostly, but also some scamp and reds make up the balance of his fish of choice. Try a live bait fish on this large hook with second choice being a whole frozen sardine.

Glenn will also rig a rod or two with a pair of smaller hooks, each tied on foot long leaders. Put two dropper loops into your line and attach snelled size 3/0 hooks. The top one should go two to three feet above the sinker and number two is right above the lead. Your sinker is a bank, not an egg, by the way. For bait, squid always works but a piece of a fillet of sardine is still my favorite. Since you are in deep water, to make sure you have a chance at still having bait on, put a little piece of squid on first and then your sardine sweetener. When finicky, the sardine strip will work like magic.

Larger fish will get hooked on this two-hook deal, but more often than not, vermilion snapper and triggerfish will beat the bigger guys to the bait. Pink porgies are another fine eating fish on this bottom, and in cold water, sea bass are on station.

You may need a pound of lead to stay in place so forget about soft rods and go with ones that have plenty of backbone. Remember that it's way, way down to the bottom.

#96 EEF SITE
Mayport

This particular reef was built by the sinking of 2,000 tons of concrete culverts in 92 feet of water back in 1990, and it didn't take

Lots of snapper like living at the EEF site!

too long before fish appeared on what used to be barren sand bottom. You may find fish in transit over sand but if you want "bottom" fish, structure is needed and thus the establishment of this fine reef by the State.

Gag grouper, gray snapper and triggerfish call EEF home. The material has a relatively low profile, only sticking eight feet off bottom, so if you haven't chartered a boat to bring you here, you will certainly need very good equipment to find the reef. Besides getting the latitude and longitude coordinates correct, you still will have to own fish-finding gear that can read bottom and tell hard from soft.

The lat reading is 3022.554 and the lon is 8057.053. The reef is pretty much a straight shot eastward out of Mayport. And 22.3 nautical miles later, you have arrived. While you may find a ramp or two somewhat back up the St. John's River, for this reef in particular, I really think that you should go with a charter skipper.

Each of the three main fish in residence have their own peculiar feeding characteristics, but all three can be caught on a size 4/0 hook baited with half of a fresh ballyhoo. Just remove the beak and tail and then cut the baitfish on a bit of an angle, from behind the gills down to just before the solid waste dump-site of the fish. Hook the head bait right through the eye sockets, and drop it down. The other half of the bait should be hooked through the tail end. When you cut bait this way, you will create a slant and therefore the bait itself will fish for you because it will leach out blood and a fresh scent.

The biggest kind of triggerfish are caught on such a bait, but grouper and snapper also will be glad to eat such an offering. The 4/0 may be a little too large for smaller triggers, but who cares. And if the steel is thick, even if a 10 pound grouper or a big snapper eats your bait, the hook should hold. I've caught fish as big as a 32 pound jack crevalle on as small a hook as a size 1/0!

Generally speaking, a longer leader may work better for mangroves (grays), but try just a three foot length and you may be able to nail some of each species. If the current is running hard, fish the stern with as light a sinker as you can hold bottom with, and be ready to stick hard and high as soon as you get slammed.

#97 HANNA PARK
Mayport

The whole name is Kathryn Abbey Hanna Park, in honor of the fine woman who gave this land to the City of Jacksonville. In fact, it's physically in Atlantic Beach, and Mayport is yet another recognizable next-door name. You can reach them at 904-249-4700.

This may be the very best "Family" location in my whole book, and that surely is a statement to make. From what I heard about it though, if not #1, it sure will come in a close second. You see, this 350 acre park has 1½ miles of wide open beach to fish from. And within the park is a nice 40 acre freshwater lake. And did I also tell you about the 293 camp sites located in the park? There's plenty of parking here.

A buck a person (age 6 and over) is all that you pay to get into the park, which stresses cleanliness and beauty. In fact, I was told that this place carries a national designation of "Blue Water Beach," meaning that it is head and shoulders above most other areas.

Let's forget about the other attractions though and talk about fishin'! A two minute walk is all you need to reach the sand! Instead of dragging your gear through deep, knee-hurting sand, four wooden beach "walkovers" are available to get you to the water. The regulars use a cart to bring their tackle to the water, via the walkovers.

In case you need bait and tackle, B & M Tackle is nearby in Atlantic Beach. (904-249-3933)

Target fish include pompano more than anything else. Live sand fleas are the best natural bait but fiddler crabs are second best for them. Use a high-low rig with just enough lead to hold you at bottom. Whiting are the second most common fish here and, as you know, they will eat anything they can fit in their mouth. A strip of squid works as will a half of a peeled shrimp. Yellowmouth trout are another fish caught from the park's beaches.

Try to hit the beach on dead low tide with waders and carefully, walk out, feeling for drop-offs. And then, if time is available, hit those spots on high tide. It is at these drop-offs that you will catch the most pompano and whiting.

#98 NASSAU SOUND AREA
South of Amelia Island

Here's an "area," rather than one specific site, courtesy of Capt. Greg Porter, who ran boats out of these waters for 20+ years before he headed north to work at Ramsey Outdoors store in Ledgewood, N. J. The "Sound" starts just south of the lower end of Amelia Island. We will soon talk about St. Mary's, etc., which is way up at the northern end of Amelia Island. This spot is down the other way.

The South Amelia River and the Nassau River form into one body and then they leave into the ocean, via Nassau Sound. And when several bodies of water clang together, they often create a fine fishery, and that is exactly what occurs here.

You can launch your boat at the bottom of the island, at A1A, and a tackle store is right there, making for quite a convenient situation. A bridge crosses over from Amelia to Little Talbot Island and very good fishing takes place just about everywhere.

There had been an old bridge sometime back that has been replaced by the newer one. But some of the old structure was left in place and quite a bit of action can be found on the old walkway.

Fishing in the confluence of the two rivers can and often does produce some of the best flounder fishing that can be found in Florida. In fact, Greg told me that the State record was caught in this area on 12/23/83, a flattie that weighed 20.9 pounds, quite a "doormat" indeed.

Come autumn, tarpon invade the inside waters as the mullet run is on. Fish for them with flies, or anchor up with live bait. Black drum are in the Sound each spring and are caught on fresh clam, live crabs, or shrimp.

Redfish are another very popular fish here and many are caught the year 'round.

Flounder fishing is done via the use of an egg sinker that is cast and retrieved. Use a barrel swivel below your slider sinker and tie in a three foot leader with a size 3/0 gold Kahle ("English) Mustad model #37162 hook. Live "mud minnows" (a/k/a killies, mummachog, minnies, etc.) are the bait of choice. Cast across current and retrieve until you feel a stop. It may not be a hard bite but you will tell the difference. Wait for a count of three and slam high. You may have been stopped by a rock, but more often, it will be a flattie! Jazz it up with a strip of squid before hooking the minnow through the lower lip.

#99 FC CULVERT SITE
Fernandina Beach

And next-to-last but not least is another of the 2,000-ton loads of culverts that were planted by the state to create yet another fine artificial reef. Several locations back, we discussed the EEF site, 2,000 tons strong, off of Mayport. Well, here's another one. There's two at 2,500 tons down a bit to the south off of St. Augustine. And way back to the northwest, off Pensacola, we have the enormous 5,700 pile called Penhall, but this one sure is pretty big.

Built in 1991, this reef is 13.6 miles out from St. Mary's Entrance in Fernandina, at latitude 3038.711, longitude 8111.242. That would take you on a south by south-east course. A boat ramp is tucked in at the west side of Fort Clinch State Park. You will be fishing offshore of the waters of Florida, but because St. Mary's marks the line that separates Georgia from Florida, you will probably see some boats from Georgia on the reef.

The water depth is 83 feet and the material has an eight foot profile. Swimming around the concrete is a variety of fish. The one that is most sought after is gray snapper. Quite a few grouper are on this bottom but there are more sheepshead than grouper.

As we have repeated often throughout this book, grouper and snapper are commonly caught on the same bait and hooks. But sheepshead, on the other hand, for a fish that sometimes reaches 10 pounds in weight, require a different style. According to a book that I checked out, *Sport Fish of the Atlantic*, the world record was better than 21 pounds, but you will need different rigs and bait for them. "Sheep-head" are more commonly known to feed much further inshore. We see them hanging around bridge and pier pilings as they pick off barnacles with their overhanging and very sharp teeth. However, they like to call artificial reefs home, especially some of the ones that offer up tasty meals off of their concrete sides like a culvert will.

Fish up a few "'grovers" and maybe a grouper or two if you can. But then try to target sheepshead. With their flat side, they will fight much harder than a tubular shaped fish does. (Close your eyes and imagine how well a one pound sunnie tussles compared to a largemouth bass, or maybe a one pound porgy in relation to a one pound snapper.)

The tough mouth of a sheepshead requires a very sharp hook to penetrate its skin. Discussed earlier, a Mustad "Virginia" bend (blue in color and used up north for blackfish) hook, model #4011E in size 4 is what works best. If you can get some small live crabs, you could wind up with a dozen of these great fighting and fine eating slabs.

#100 ST. MARY'S INLET
Fernandina Beach

Way back up the northeast coast is this, the northeast corner of the State of Florida. In fact, the jetty on the north side of the inlet is in Georgia! And the south side, therefore, is where we will tell you about now, in detail.

The inlet is ¾ of a mile wide and is very active. In fact, a submarine base is reached upriver via the inlet. All kinds of big boat traffic come into this inlet so a word to the wise is something we must give you. Don't try to anchor in the inlet in a small boat, and for that matter, don't even drift in it unless your engine is either in idle or ready to crank up in a hurry, for obvious reasons.

The south jetty is over a mile long and a fine pier can be found here. The facility is called Fort Clinch State Park and Pier (904-261-4212) and the number at the marina is 904-491-2090. There's plenty of parking available in the park. You might want to book a small boat charter at the marina instead of giving it a go via your own craft, at least until you get used to the water here.

Fishing from the jetty as well as the pier involves a wide variety of species. They include whiting and croaker from spring through fall, along with bluefish. The style for all three involves the use of bait. Try peeled shrimp for the first two but a chunk of fresh and smelly fish is best for blues. Go with a wired hook to avoid being chopped off by the toothsome blue devils. Fishing close in to the rocks on high tide will produce some nice sheepshead but be sure you have a sturdy rod to drag the fish out of the rough bottom. This also applies from the pier when 90% of your sheepshead will be caught within a few feet of a piling.

Spanish mackerel come flying over the pier's rail as well as the jetty from spring through summer, with small jigs working best for them.

The tide can cook in the inlet so try to fish during slower water conditions. The last two hours of outgoing and the first of incoming are best. Also try the high-water change of tide when the water slows for second best action.

If you are fishing from a boat make certain you know what rules apply to both states, Florida, as well as Georgia, just in case you are fishing on the north side of the inlet.

King mackerel come charging into the mouth and are caught with lures as well as live bait. Spaniards, flounder, red drum, and speckled trout all are taken from boats. And if your rod bends way, way over, that could be a big black drum at the other end. Last but not least are the wonderful fighting fish, jack crevalle, fun to catch but not to eat.

In closing, I hope you found this book both interesting and informative. My intent was to tell fishermen from Florida, as well as those who may want to head to this great state, just what kinds of fishing are available to them, from one end of the saltwater areas of the state to the other. And if you think I may have come somewhat close to achieving my goal, then look forward to the next book, which will be about freshwater!

PS: You may have seen reference to a three-hook set up quite often in the book. Whether it involves a bucktail jig that has two tag hooks added on, or a plain hook that I add two more behind, let's go over how to set this up. Clearly, I didn't invent this deal, but since I learned how to do it from some real experts, I thought you might want to learn how to do it.

When using a bucktail jig, simply have a few extra plain hooks at the ready. When the fish are small, they will be size 1/0. For bigger fish, I use a 3/0. Make sure your jig has a strong, relatively thick hook shank, not one of those skinny freshwater models. Your added hook will slide right out of the eye of the next hook, more often than not, with a freshwater jig hook.

Okay, got a bunch of jigs and loose hooks? Open the eye of several hooks with a good pair of wire cutters. Do this by pressing the points of the wire cutters into the eye opening, and with practice, you will be able to create a little widening at the opening. Now stick the point of your jig's hook into the eye and through it. Then take a good pair of heavy pliers and close the opening of the

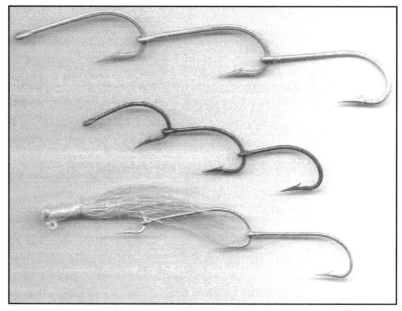

7/0, 4/0 and bucktail – triple hook set-ups.

bare hook's eye so that it won't allow the jig hook to drop out. Tricky, but if I can do it, you sure can too. Repeat this with another loose hook, and when done correctly, you will be able to drape a sardine fillet (or other strip bait) across each of the three hooks. Do it right and the bait will flutter in the water and you will have each barb in the strike zone.

And a variation of this style will work just as well for plain hooks. You may be after king mackerel with long shank size silver 7/0 hooks or maybe yellowtail snappers with size 4/0 short shank bronze ones. The idea is that you can hang a whole bait fish, sardine, ballyhoo, whatever, on this set-up and, again, have three points ready to stick whatever eats your bait. Again, open the eye of one hook and stick another barb into the opening and shut the eye with your pliers. Do this a second time and you will have three hooks that a long baitfish can be draped across. Some guys bury the top two barbs into the baitfish's back and the hook that is tied to your line is made to penetrate the tail end of the bait. Others bring the barb through the back flesh with the first two hooks and then through the tail end with the hook that is tied to your line. It's different strokes for different folks but for sure, this system give you a much better chance at hooking up, and not getting cut off as often as when you only use a single hook set-up. You can use this rig while anchor fishing, but you may need it even more on a drift to avoid short bites.

Scuze me, gone fishin'

Index

About The Author

Manny Luftglass has written his column, "Gone Fishin'" for a wide variety of newspapers since 1971. This is his 13th book. Two were published by Rutgers University Press and he self-published all eleven others, including this one.

His credentials include being published in dozens of newspapers, plus feature articles in *The Anglers News, East Coast Angler, The Fisherman Magazine, The Fisherman's Trader, Skylands Visitor, Carpworld* (England), and its equivalent in Germany, *North American Fisherman, Sportsmen's Series, Fishing & Hunting News, Nick Jr.,* and *Aging With Style.*

Order Form

For additional copies of this book, any of the eleven other *Gone Fishin'* books, or my book, *So You Want To Write A Book,* please send check or money order to:

Gone Fishin' Enterprises
PO Box 556
Annandale, NJ 08801

- New Jersey residents please add 6% state sales tax.
- Tell me who you'd like the book autographed to.
- There will no shipping or handling charges.

For bulk orders call: 908 996-2145

Look up *Gone Fishin'* books at:
www.gonefishinbooks.com

Name: _____

Address: _____

City: _____ State: _____ Zip: _____

Autograph To: _____

Please send me:

# of Copies	Book Title	Price
_____	Gone Fishin'... With Kids	$ 9.99
_____	Gone Fishin'... In Spruce Run Reservoir	$12.95
_____	Gone Fishin'... For Carp	$12.95
_____	**Gone Fishin'... Florida's 100 Best Salt Waters**	**$13.95**
_____	Gone Fishin'... For Beginners	$13.95
_____	So You Want To Write A Book	$13.95
_____	Gone Fishin'... In Round Valley Reservoir	$13.95
_____	Gone Fishin'... In Lake Hopatcong	$13.95
_____	Gone Fishin'... The 50 Best Waters In Pennsylvania	$13.95
_____	Gone Fishin'... The 75 Best Waters In Connecticut	$13.95
_____	Gone Fishin'... In N.J. Saltwater Rivers And Bays	$14.95
_____	Gone Fishin'... The 100 Best Spots In New Jersey	$16.00
_____	Gone Fishin'... The 100 Best Spots In New York	$16.00